REQUIEM, RWANDA

REQUIEM,
RWANDA

Laura Apol

MICHIGAN STATE UNIVERSITY PRESS ▪ *East Lansing*

⊗ The paper used in this publication meets the minimum requirements
of ANSI/NISO Z39.48-1992 (R 1997) (Permanence of Paper).

 Michigan State University Press
East Lansing, Michigan 48823-5245

Printed and bound in the United States of America.

21 20 19 18 17 16 15   1 2 3 4 5 6 7 8 9 10

Library of Congress Control Number: 2014941665
ISBN: 978-1-61186-158-7 (pbk.)
ISBN: 978-1-60917-444-6 (ebook: PDF)
ISBN: 978-1-62895-136-3 (ebook: ePub)
ISBN: 978-1-62896-136-2 (ebook: Kindle)

Book design by Charlie Sharp, Sharp Des!gns, Lansing, Michigan
Cover design by Erin Kirk New
Cover art is "Rwanda Souls" ©Fern Seiden 2014 and is used with permission.
All rights reserved.

g green press Michigan State University Press is a member of the Green Press
INITIATIVE Initiative and is committed to developing and encouraging
ecologically responsible publishing practices. For more information about the
Green Press Initiative and the use of recycled paper in book publishing, please
visit *www.greenpressinitiative.org*.

Visit Michigan State University Press on the World Wide Web at
www.msupress.org

I will not praise amnesia
—GEORGE ROCHBERG

CONTENTS

ix   FOREWORD

xiii   PREFACE

xv   PROLOGUE: A BRIEF HISTORY OF RWANDA

INTROIT

3   Genesis: The Source of the Nile

DIES IRAE

9   Early April in Rwanda

11   Six Seconds

13   Even the Land Did Not Escape

14   Canticle for the Bones of the Dead

15   Genocide Site 1: Nyamata Church

16   Genocide Site 2: Ntarama Church

18   Eucharist

19   Mother of God

21   Church at Nyange

LACRIMOSA

25   Witness

26   Rift

28   The Lives of Others

30   Left

31   Pink

33   Confession

34   Return to Remera

35   Dry Bones

SANCTUS

39   At the Hotel Bar

40   Watching a Man Cut the Grass

41 Lifelines

42 Before Memorial Week: April 5, 2009

44 Poolside after Dark

45 Testimony

46 Meeting François in Heaven

47 Samuel and the Boys

49 Gorilla Family *Amahoro*

51 *Umuganda*

52 Reparations

53 Rwanda Stands up for Haiti: January 2010

55 Language Lessons

BENEDICTUS

61 Milkfugue

63 NOTES ON THE POEMS

71 EPILOGUE: WRITER AS WITNESS

91 NOTES

95 ADDITIONAL RESOURCES

99 ACKNOWLEDGMENTS

FOREWORD

Laura Apol's meditation in poetry form on the Rwandan genocide and its legacy, together with her notes and commentary on her witness during and after years she taught testimony writing in Rwanda, offers a startling and remarkable original document. I have seen few things like it. I am neither a student of poetry nor of the Rwandan genocide, but I am a student of genocide and an aficionado of testimony, memory, and witness after catastrophe. I sense a special talent and extraordinary bond with Rwanda at work in these pages.

Normally poems in poetry books stand alone; they are offered by the writer unmediated. Here a brief prologue provides important background and context; notes on the poems plus an epilogue explore the process by which the poems came to be. A reader who studies the poems, reads the notes and commentary, and then returns to the poems again will be twice rewarded.

Laura Apol writes just enough in this slim volume, and in the right kinds of ways, to permit readers to enter the space of remembrance with her and to come to know many things as she does. She approaches her subject in a searching, humble way. "This is no place for me," she worries self-consciously. She is a traveler-outsider, a white Midwestern female without deep roots or experience in the African Great Lakes region. And yet this *umuzungu* writes evocatively as a knowing and sensitive witness about nation, church, and history in Africa, about the ruins of bones and skulls in Rwanda, and about the mass graves and terrible night dreams that coexist with Rwanda's beautiful landscape and lovely thousand hills.

Like her reaction to a man she encounters on a plane, a man deeply scarred, part of his body appearing as if it had been gouged out, a man returned from the dead, the writer cannot look directly at the genocide: it is too horrific. She does not write about its development, nor the role of international actors. She offers no analytic account of the cataclysm's causes. And yet she cannot look away either. She cannot help but see it and its outcomes everywhere. Nor can the reader be permitted to look away. The outsider-witness draws it all into her and expresses it feelingly and knowledgeably in an original poetry of witness, a form of art and social engagement.

Laura Apol reminds us that Europe is deeply implicated. The colonial heritage, the identity cards, the reified categories, then the horrific, knowing, inexcusable refusal to intervene or engage in rescue, even to call the genocide by its name—she captures all this in a sustained lament. She draws on Glori's story to take us into the heart of the darkness; she tells how mass killing is done—"*six seconds* / to chop a limb, slice an artery." She also registers the failures of justice after the genocide and up to the present. Despite the processes set in place to aid conciliation, Rwanda remains a bloodstained land of loss, a place of "sharp thorns" beneath the forgiving surface. Even the memorials amount largely to making an uneasy peace with the past rather than truly confronting and mastering it.

Real or actual memorials, as distinct from the planned memorials, exist all over the nation, scattered like the mattresses Laura Apol sees in Samuel's home for fatherless boys. They exist in the ruins of numberless churches; they exist in the names the young bride Mukundwa recites at night. They also exist in the efforts of Laura Apol's Rwandan colleagues to "write" the genocide to find their lost selves. I look forward to learning more from the mass of coming testimonies.

A few decades ago, Claude Lanzmann remarked about the absence of a "presence" about the Holocaust in European cultural life; his film *Shoah* was his herculean effort to restore a sense of that presence. Laura Apol employs her own art to find and explore elements of the past in present Rwanda and to highlight the lingering pain and unfinished suffering. Like the man from Ernest's story who hears the voices of the children in his head, she hears many lingering voices as she returns again and again to post-genocide Rwanda.

I want to emphasize that the notes on the poems are indispensable and help deepen our appreciation. The section on the writer as witness also frames the enterprise and helps us see it whole. It tells what brought her to Rwanda initially, highlighting the writer's interest in a project using writing for therapeutic purposes, and indicates how her ties with Rwandans and with Rwanda deepened and brought her back as a friend and witness. She writes of numerous attempts to translate emotions into words. She shifts her gaze, focusing on her own witness as well as the unhealed wounds of Rwanda. Increasingly, she names her mission as providing a new "poetry of witness," an effort through personal discovery and creative art to help others see and understand how "the past [in Rwanda] and the present are inextricably intertwined."

Laura Apol's discussion of the writing project she spearheaded and of the uses of writing to heal wounded lives reminds me of experiments with writing (also with drawing) that others pioneered in group homes in Europe after World War II where Holocaust orphans and youths were gathered. Those others, too, were outsiders, in the sense that they had no idea what human experience had been in the extreme conditions of the Nazi camps. Yet these men and women were open to hearing the stories, exploring people's losses and lingering traumas, and they provided young survivors with safe opportunities to express their experiences and begin to reintegrate torn lives.

In sum, this is a startlingly original interdisciplinary work that builds in power across its sections. Laura Apol explores what it means to be a witness writer and to express her witness as art. She probes the challenges to witnessing as an outsider and also wrestles with the difficulties of turning suffering into poetry. At the same time, she offers feeling commentary on the legacies of genocide in a distant country she knows well now twenty years after the events.

PREFACE

On my desk is a drawing: yellow construction paper, thick markers and crayons. There is an orange sun and a square house with a peaked roof. There is grass that undulates like waves, and a flower the size of a tree floating on the rippling green surface like a boat. There is a central human figure, too, with a broad smile, circles for feet, arms spread up to the sky, and hands that look remarkably like five-pointed stars. The drawing is signed at the bottom, in careful letters—some reversed, all haphazardly spaced: JOSEPH. *It is a drawing filled with joy, a child's love of life. It is a drawing that almost did not exist.*

Joseph is the son of Glori. Glori is the daughter of Rose. Glori and Rose are survivors of genocide. Though he is only six, Joseph is the reason for this book—the Joseph whose artwork smiles at me each morning from my desk, and all the Josephs growing up, or never to grow up, in Rwanda.

Rwanda is a country of children who dream and draw—some with families, some without. And it is a country of children whose dreams have been lost—children who did not survive, and children without childhoods who did; orphans left to fend for themselves; family lines that will never go on.

The poems in this collection provide an account of my experience of Rwanda, where—as Joseph depicted—there are orange suns, thick-walled houses, waves of green grass and flowering trees. The poems speak of the people I met and my learning about the country: its history, the effects of white colonialism, the 1994 genocide that—far too late—caught the attention of the world, and the halting, incomplete, sometimes horrible and often astonishing moving forward of the nation, the people, and the land.

I made my first trip to Rwanda in 2006. The initial goal was to develop, with Rwandan and American colleagues, a project using narrative writing to facilitate healing among survivors of the 1994 genocide against the Tutsi. A poet myself, I view writing as a form of social action; I believe words have important work to do in the world. As a result, while I was in Rwanda leading writing workshops for others, I felt moved to write my own poetry as well. After the writing-for-healing project ended, I returned—a half dozen times, usually for several weeks—to take notes and draft poems.

These poems are the result of those many visits spanning many years. It was impossible to spend time in Rwanda, engaging with survivors, without recognizing the weight of history—on the people, on the land itself, and in the churches, the schools, and the memorials. The genocide is present in many of the poems. However, my primary goal for this work has not been to focus on the genocide, but rather to present an account of my own relationships with and understandings of people *post*-genocide—how they re-enter their lives, where their stories go, and how a country that has been deeply wounded by its history continues on. As an outside witness, I have felt a need to put my observations and experiences into words.

In any writing of witness, there is not only what is being witnessed, but also the individual bearing witness. The poems express my developing awareness of the complications of being a white woman, a Westerner, and a writer in such a context: my sense of compassion, privilege, horror, guilt, voyeurism, obligation, and love.

Most of the poems can be read with only a basic knowledge of the social and political context of Rwanda. Others require greater familiarity with Rwandan culture, language, and history. To assist readers in this understanding, I have provided in the prologue a brief overview of the history of Rwanda. There are translations of Kinyarwanda words and lengthier explanatory notes available at the end of the book. Additional resources are listed at the back of the book to encourage further reading about Rwanda. In the epilogue, an account of the writing-for-healing work and a history of the writing of the poems is provided to create a greater context for the collection.

PROLOGUE: A BRIEF HISTORY OF RWANDA

The country of Rwanda is located in east central Africa, two degrees south of the equator and bordered by Tanzania, Uganda, Burundi, and the Democratic Republic of Congo. Breathtakingly beautiful, it is known as "Le Pays des Mille Collines"—The Land of a Thousand Hills—and the elevation of those hills makes it temperate year round. Historically, its people flourished with cattle and farming, developing a culturally rich society that was ruled by a central monarch (*mwami*) and sophisticated networks drawn along lines of regions and clans, divided into a standardized structure of provinces, districts, hills, and neighborhoods, and administered by a hierarchy of chiefs. Since precolonial times, Rwanda has been a unified state, with well-established borders and a centralized military structure, and the population is drawn from one ethnic and linguistic group.[1]

European explorers viewed this small, densely populated area with little interest; the country had no diamonds, oil, or gold. Landlocked, Rwanda did not become a major source of slaves. Without these resources to entice outsiders, the country remained relatively unknown and undisturbed throughout the decades of European interest in exploring "the dark continent."

Rwanda did occasionally appear on the political maps of Europe. When the region was divided by European powers in the 1884 Berlin Conference, Rwanda became part of German East Africa. In 1892, the first European (Austrian cartographer Oscar Baumann) came to Rwanda as part of his study of the area, and the German explorer Count Gustav von Götzen, who later became the governor of German East Africa, arrived two years later. Near the end of the nineteenth century, European explorers crossed Rwanda in their search for the source of the Nile, and European missionaries ("The White Fathers")[2] came after, bringing to the country their version of God. Following WWI, Rwanda passed from Germany to Belgium as the result of a League of Nations mandate—a concession for defeat and a prize for victory—and in the years that ensued, Belgian officials put into place a system of colonial administration that

xv

lasted until Rwanda's independence in 1962. For the most part, though, Rwanda was considered to be of little economic or strategic importance to the West and thus was mostly ignored. From the early 1960s until 1994, Rwanda only occasionally surfaced in the Western media as a troubled African nation, beset by ethnic conflict and instability.

But ethnic conflict was not always the case. When Europeans arrived in Rwanda, they recorded within the people three groups: Hutu, Tutsi, and Twa.[3] For much of the precolonial history of the country, the two major classifications, Hutu and Tutsi,[4] had been terms used to indicate economic status among people who spoke the same language, inter-married, and worked and worshipped side by side. Within this system, Hutu (the majority) were farmers and Tutsi (the minority) were owners of cattle. The two groups existed in a client-patron contract called the *ubuhake*—a feudal-type class system through which the Hutu indentured themselves to a Tutsi lord, providing agricultural products and personal service in exchange for the use of cattle and land. Within this arrangement, the positions of Hutu and Tutsi were markers of economic and social class rather than ethnicity, and thus they were fluid and permeable, breached by changes in fortune, re-alignments through marriage, and economic success.

Rwandan rule was similarly constructed. At the apex of the class system was the king—the *mwami*—who governed through a complicated system of family lines and alliances. In this way, Rwandan rule was determined by clan, class, and lineage, primarily (though not exclusively) within the Tutsi minority. Political clashes were by clan, class, and lineage as well, and although there was conflict between the few with power and the majority without, the tension was not ethnic and was never characterized by systemic racialized violence.

With the arrival of European powers, however, the use of the terms *Hutu* and *Tutsi* as group markers shifted. As a result of European influence, these designations became reified into ethnic designations, signifying fixed categories rather than a distinction that could be traversed by marriage or changes of economic fortune. Identity cards were issued in the early 1930s, further concretizing the notions of *Hutu* and *Tutsi* as fixed ethnic markers. Once the fluid terms *Hutu* and *Tutsi* had been re-interpreted as unchanging ethnic identities, an ethnicity-based hierarchy was put into place by the European leaders, almost always favoring the Tutsi, aligning European powers with existing Tutsi rulers and resulting in increased Hutu-Tutsi conflict that was supported and often fueled by the European heads.

In 1962, pressured by anticolonial democratic sentiment, Belgium shifted alliance within Rwanda. Perhaps partly in an effort to punish the Tutsi rulers who were pressing for autonomy, Belgian officials turned against the leaders with whom they had previously aligned themselves, handing over power to the Hutu majority before granting the country its independence. Ethnic designations continued to be exploited by leaders who perpetuated an ideology of difference and a culture of fear; Hutu—who once had been oppressed—now became the powerful oppressors. Decades of ethnic conflict followed. Early massacres of Tutsi at the hands of Hutu officials led thousands of Tutsi to flee to nearby countries, where they lived in camps and where, eventually, rebel groups made up of the refugees and the sons of the refugees formed the Rwandan Patriotic Front (RPF)[5] and periodically staged invasions across the borders, demanding a return to the country to which they belonged. In retaliation, the Hutu government launched a series of ethnic purges within Rwanda, in which thousands of Tutsi were killed—rehearsals for a more major event in the planning, and tests to determine whether and how the international community would intervene.[6] Despite evidence that these government-sanctioned retaliatory moves were ethnically motivated, targeting civilians (including the elderly, women, and children), the international community did nothing, emboldening the planners to prepare for a larger-scale event,[7] convincing the Rwandans—Hutu and Tutsi alike—that no future international intervention would be forthcoming.

In 1990, the Rwandan Civil War began when the RPF invaded northern Rwanda. Though the attempt to overthrow the government failed, RPF successes on the battlefield led to forced peace negotiations and the August 1993 signing of the Arusha Accords by then-President Juvénal Habyarimana—a move intended to create a power-sharing government. However, the Arusha Accords inflamed radical Hutu, who had no intention of sharing power with Tutsi, and intensified support for the "Hutu Power" movement. Extremists within Rwanda's political elite blamed the entire Tutsi population for the country's increasing social, economic, and political woes, convincing ordinary Hutu citizens that power-sharing with Tutsi would lead to the "re-enslavement" of Hutu at Tutsi hands. Progress toward peace was stalled.

Then, at 8:30 P.M. on April 6, 1994, President Habyarimana's plane was shot down over Kigali as he was returning from Tanzania. The President and all others on board were killed, and in the hours that followed, the Hutu government launched what may have been the most efficient genocide of modern history, in which ordinary citizens were mobilized to kill their neighbors, coworkers, family members, and friends. At first, only highly visible Tutsi and politically "moderate" Hutu who supported the multi-party democracy or who resisted genocide ideology were killed. Eventually, all Tutsi became targets, as were Hutu who refused to participate in the genocide, who hid or defended Tutsi, who were perceived to be Tutsi, or who were linked to Tutsi through marriage, friendship, or family lines.

If for most of its history Rwanda was largely invisible to the West, the eruption of a genocide of this type and proportion eventually caught the attention of the world. Between early April and mid-July 1994, in the span of one hundred days, eight hundred thousand (perhaps as many as a million)[8] Rwandan Tutsi and politically "moderate" Hutu were killed by their neighbors, relatives, and friends—most with ordinary implements of house and field: knives, machetes, garden hoes, sticks, and clubs. Much of the killing occurred in homes and in the countryside; much also occurred in churches, promoted by church leaders who at times organized, at times participated in, and who often were unwilling or unable to prevent the massacres that took place. Whereas in earlier ethnicity-based killings in Rwanda, churches and schools had been places of refuge and safety, during the 1994 genocide Tutsi were encouraged by government officials to gather in these locations, then were murdered en masse—sometimes with guns or grenades, sometimes by hand, and sometimes through razing the building or setting it on fire with the living (at times numbering in the thousands) inside.

For the most part, the international community stood by as the killing took place. The RPF, moving across the country from Uganda in the northeast, eventually stopped the genocide, but not until approximately three-quarters of the Tutsi in Rwanda—and thousands of Hutu who opposed the genocide—had been killed.[9]

It was later claimed by Western leaders that no one understood the magnitude of what was taking place inside the Rwandan borders, but the Western world knew. And it looked away. There is evidence that the United States and the United Nations deliberately ignored clear and compelling information about the escalating violence in Rwanda, both before and during the genocide—withholding aid, refusing to intervene, and even reducing the peacekeeping forces that could have served as a deterrent.[10] France actively supported the extremist Hutu government, supplying weapons and training, and, through *Opération Turquoise*, creating in the final weeks of the genocide a "safe zone" in the southwest of Rwanda that was publicly proposed as a means to provide sanctuary for Tutsi refugees, but that in fact allowed Hutu *génocidaires* to escape from the RPF into what was then western Zaire (now the Democratic Republic of Congo).[11]

After one hundred days of unimaginable violence, Rwandans were left to reconstruct what was left of their lives and their communities. Of a population of seven million, nearly one million were dead and an additional one and a quarter million had become refugees (a quarter of a million Tutsi fled to Tanzania during the genocide, and a million Hutu fled to Zaire at the genocide's end). The country was in shambles: fields were untended and businesses were closed; schools and churches were abandoned; entire villages were destroyed. Children were traumatized—orphaned, homeless, and physically and psychologically scarred. They had been victims of, forced participants in, or witnesses to unspeakable violence.[12]

In the years that followed, a slow rebuilding took place. Bodies were gathered, identified (when possible), and buried. Mass graves were excavated, and memorial sites were created in the churches and schools where massacres had taken place. Many of those who had fled in the years before the genocide returned to the country. Children without parents were placed with relatives, with families in the community, or in homes headed by other children.[13]

The government outlawed identity cards. Hutu and Tutsi once more lived side by side—shopped in the same markets, walked the same roads, and attended the same schools. Local tribunals (called *gacaca*) were estab-lished to help survivors experience some sense of justice,[14] and genocide planners were tried at the International Criminal Tribunal for Rwanda (ICTR) in Arusha, Tanzania.[15] The country moved forward, constructing businesses, homes, streets, schools, hospitals, hotels, restaurants, and related infrastructure to support an influx of expats and foreigners.

Yet each year, during the first week of April—the start of the rainy season in Rwanda—the nation stops to remember. To confront its own demons. To try, in whatever ways possible, to make peace with the past.

To find rest—*requiem*—not only for the dead, but for the living as well.

REQUIEM,
RWANDA

INTROIT

Genesis: The Source of the Nile

Twin tributaries, the Blue Nile and White Nile
flow north, merge to birth the sacred
river. Its floods are the key to life:
even seasons follow the river's flow.
The Nile separates East and West;
each day, the sun lives, dies—
traverses the underworld to be resurrected
in dawn. And so the river is passage:
in each tomb, a boat to ferry the soul beyond.

But what is the great Nile's source,
farthest point from which the river arrives?
No one can locate the river's head;
no maps contain the womb
from which the mighty waters are born.
The Blue Nile's birth site is the first
to be discovered: topsoil from Tana, rich silt
flowing downstream from that Ethiopian lake.
The White Nile, longer branch, maintains mystery—
headwaters breaking in a deep, unknowable core.

2.

John Hanning Speke, British explorer, sought
the White Nile's source. He found in East Africa
a vast expanse of open water, answered the question
with a lake, named it for his queen. *The Nile is settled,*
he telegraphed home. So many ways to be wrong.

John Hanning Speke, British explorer, sought
the black Africans' source, turned to Genesis,
claimed those with dark skin were children of Ham,

Noah's sinful son, cursed by the Father
and destined to be slaves. Then, in Rwanda,
Speke encountered Tutsi—light-skinned, thin-lipped,
a cause for revision. *Ethiopian*, he declared;
descendants of milk-white Shem darkened
through coupling with descendants of Ham—
interlopers to Rwanda's fertile hills.

3.

Richard Kandt, German explorer, founded
Kigali, though it had already been founded
for five hundred years—*umurwa mukuru,*
the ruling *mwami's* seat. History, measured
in imperial years, marks origins from the arrival
of colonial skin.

Of much Kandt was sure. Of this he was not:
Caput Nili—the Head of the Nile. *Is Lake Victoria
the true source of the Nile*, he asked, *or merely
a rest in its flow?* Kandt's answer: a spring
rising beneath his feet in the forests of Rwanda.
(A royal nurse puts a seed in a new infant's hand,
and the next king has been born.) Kandt's spring
becomes a stream, becomes the Nyabarongo—
flows north into the pregnant pause of Lake Victoria.
Genesis of the Nile: Kandt rewrote the river's beginning,
and it was good.

4.

Within Rwanda, these things become Truth:
Speke's origin of the people, Kandt's origin of the Nile.
Hutu are ordered to fill the Nyabarongo with corpses,

float them back to the country from which they came.
Ethiopia can welcome those interlopers home.

The Nyabarongo feeds the Lake, the Lake feeds
the Nile, and the Kenyan government bans
fishing on Lake Victoria. *Fish*, they say, *are feeding
on human flesh.* Cut open a fish: Tutsi fingers, toes.

     5.

Thus it was proved: Lake Victoria was not
the source of the Nile. Thus it was proved: Tutsi bodies
could be returned to their mythic home. The widening river
would carry them along.

One unnamed stream leads to another,
to Nyabarongo and the great flooding Nile.
No boat to the afterlife; no resurrection
with the sun. This is genesis—origin, source.

So many ways to be wrong.

DIES IRAE

Early April in Rwanda

Somewhere a woman is cooking beans.
    Her yard is quiet, the baby asleep

        on her back. She hums
        as she moves about the fire,

        breathing the familiar comfort
        of wood smoke, watching color bleed

        from clouds above the hills—
        the last moment between daylight

        and dark. Her legs fold beneath her
        as she crouches, milk-filled breasts shifting

        as she leans to stir the pot. This red dirt
        is what she knows, these hibiscus

        and nightshades in bloom. Next week
        the baby will be baptized: Charles, Claude,

        or Jean-Pierre. Time will tell his name,
        and she is listening.

Somewhere a man is making a machete
    so sharp it can split pineapple,

        hack cane, or sever the limb
        of the acacia. He loves the last light

        on the road, on the blade, on the plot
        of hard earth that will always be his.

Somewhere a flower falls from a flowering
tree. Each takes it as a sign:

the days of rain are about to begin.

Six Seconds

One hundred days, one million people:
ten thousand deaths per day.

The killers consider it a job:
Gukora akazi, they say to each other;
Kujya ku kazi, to their wives.

They work by day, sleep at night.
The job requires speed,
so they press on.

Ten thousand a day,
fifteen-hour days—
that's 666 per hour:
the mark of the beast.
Round down.

Six hundred per hour,
ten per minute,

six seconds

to chop a limb, slice an artery,
start the graveward journey with rape,

to pile stones on the living,
force a husband to kill a wife,
or a woman her child,

to pour gasoline, strike the match.

Breathe in, breathe out—one is dead;

breathe in, breathe out—another.

Every six seconds

for one hundred
interminable
days.

Even the Land Did Not Escape

What the grass witnessed,
what the water absorbed,
what the rocks took in, remains.

Even the air remembers. Even the rain.

There were tears in the red dirt,
rivers running with blood.
Bodies bloated on the lakes.
Flowers opened, closed, fell.

All around, the scars of erosion,
ghosts of mahogany and fir.

In those hundred days
did anyone notice the terraced hills,
see the land alive with beauty and food?

Could anyone love the late slant of dusk,
the clear sea of stars,
praise the dawn, seeping
crimson across the sky?

Canticle for the Bones of the Dead

mass
grave

when the cantor sings
      who sings back

separated from your name

the voice that is yours is scattered
      marrow dried to dust

yet
I believe

you have something
to say

Genocide Site 1: Nyamata Church

Nyamata
means *place of milk.*

In this room, piles of clothes.
Bullet holes in the ceiling and walls.

Blood on the altar,

a glass box of rosaries,
preserved like the priests
who chose safety and fled.

The niche for the Host
is open, empty; God,

nowhere to be found.

Rows of fractured bones,
form a mute congregation
in this place of milk
and horror.

Broken bodies, shed blood,
but not those of a Savior—

not in this Golgotha, this God-
forsaken
place of the skull.

Genocide Site 2: Ntarama Church

If Jesus had been there,
he would have fed the five thousand
with loaves and fishes.
Blessed are those, he would have said,

> *who hunger and thirst for righteousness*
> *for they shall be filled.*

As it was, they brought provisions of their own—
dishes, utensils, cooking pots now stored
in the sorting room, numbered and placed in piles:
dolls, hairbrushes,

> *Blessed are the poor in spirit*
> *for theirs is the kingdom of God*

eyeglasses, a pocket knife. Between the pews,
the bodies—all killed by hand—lie where they fell.
The aisles are littered with skeletons, handbags,
and toys. Tatters of clothing

> *Blessed are the meek*
> *for they shall inherit the earth*

rot on the bones. Jaws, pelvises,
rows of teeth. Bones of the hand, bones of the feet—
each day someone sorts them:
hip bone, thigh bone, thigh bone,

> *Blessed are those who are persecuted for justice's sake*
> *for theirs is the Kingdom of Heaven*

knee bone. The Stations of the Cross

span the front of the church—
Jesus grows weary, Jesus bleeds on the cross,
Jesus' body is wrapped in linens

> *Blessed are those who mourn*
> *for they shall be comforted*

and laid in the tomb. Outside, a sign:
"If you know yourself and you know me,
you could not kill me."
What does it mean to know

> *Blessed are the merciful*
> *for they shall be shown mercy*

and be known? And what can be known
of these nameless remains
—the last prayers spoken, the last words
uttered by killer, victim,

> *Blessed are the pure in heart*
> *for they shall see God*

parent, child? This church *is* sanctuary now;
it holds once more its silence, holds its prayers:
the cattle in the distance,
the child at the gate,

> *Blessed are the peacemakers*
> *for they shall be called the children of God*

the cooing of doves. The rooster's crow.

Eucharist

has always been about betrayal—
the Judas kiss before death.

Some priests were complicit, they say,
offering shelter

then opening doors
for the killers to come in.

One blessed the bread
then unlocked the gate:

I have other Christians.
You can have these.

Mother of God

As if rape were not enough,
they did it with a spear.

As if a spear were not enough,
they thrust so hard
the point pierced her skull.

As if her ruptured skull were not enough,
they did it with her baby
tied to her back,

then nailed the living baby
to her shattered body
with a sharpened stick.

In the church,
the mother-child skeleton,
a spear run through, remains;

the blessed Virgin,
looking on, remains
untouched.

Mother of God—

speak to me of crucifixion
and I will tell you about the human body
becoming a cross.

I will ask what can save
or be saved

when we choose not to look,
hear the story, weep and forget,

when we refuse to inhabit these bones.

Church at Nyange

> By faith the walls of Jericho fell down
> after they had been encircled for seven days.
>   —HEBREWS 11:30

You know the story:
a march around the city, trumpets blowing,
walls tumbling down,
God's enemies beneath the rubble,

and a scarlet cord from an upstairs window
to show which house should be saved.

At the church at Nyange
there was also a week of siege,
interahamwe circling, whistles and drums,
thousands of Tutsi inside

and a priest who jeered,
Where is the Tutsi God now?
before ordering bulldozers to work;

a priest sipping banana beer
as the walls came down,
the steeple remaining,
God's children beneath the rubble;

a priest with a rifle,
firing from the steeple window
at those who tried to flee.

There are believers all over the world,
he proclaimed to the dying

and the dead. *I can destroy this house*
and they will rebuild it in three days.

The church at Nyange
is now a grave-studded ruin,
but the priest resurrected himself
in Europe, where the church universal
took him in,

because faith is a brick
that builds a house,
a beam that, falling,
crushes everything beneath.

Yes, you know the story.
So where is the Tutsi God now?

At night, you sleep under a cascade of net,
a stone for your pillow, each dream
a hard waterfall shaped like a steeple—

bright blood in the rushing, a ribbon
that breaks into brilliant red birds.

Around you, doves tumble down,
their stunned promise drowned
in a scarlet sea.

LACRIMOSA

Witness

I write your story
on bones.

I write your story on bones
and skulls. On bones and skulls
and teeth.

I write your story in tears
not my own.

If I lift my foot,
you will see the sole
stained with your blood.
Where my words go
they leave a scabby trail.

No horrors haunt
my sleep; no swollen dogs
pace my empty rooms.

I cannot reach your aching
phantom limbs.

I tell your story in a voice white
as bone—a voice white

as bones, skulls, and teeth.

Rift

1.

From the sky,
this land of a thousand hills
is a place of beauty:

arteries of red-burnt road,
patchwork greens that ring and rise
along the hills, the great rift
valley and rivers carved
through dappled groves
of bananas and palms.

What is there here for me,
umuzungu who watches with words
a country once torn, beginning
to heal?

This is no place for me.

2.

The plane touches down, rolls to a stop,
and the man two rows ahead rises
to face me—tall, sturdy, thick.
A giant of a man. He turns to leave:

a man with a scar.

Six inches across, two inches wide,
a full inch deep,
it runs the width of his neck
at the base of his skull.

The tissue is shiny, stretched,
mottled white against dark scalp.

Scar is not the word.
It is part of his body gouged out,
a pound of flesh gone, a visible absence
—skin, muscle, bone.

He is a man come back from the dead.

I cannot look; I cannot look
away.

The Lives of Others

Nothing is only itself:

in each brick, a story
of mud, grass, and sun,
in each tree, a story
reaching back to its roots.

The seed of the avocado
carries out to the world
what its leaves have taken in,

a young girl hides a coin
in the oleander, saying aloud
her wish, her prayer, her incantation
of rage.

Note the curved flute of the calla lily—
how it rings the flower's center
like the scar around the sightless eye
of Jean de Dieu

who each morning brings
coffee, milk, and two
hard-boiled eggs.

Murakoze, I say—
to the flower, to the man,
to the milk and eggs.

Murakoze to the brick
and tree and buttery fruit.

Murakoze to the girl
bent over the bush's begging hands.

But I mean to say more.
I mean to say this:
each story holds a question
that is more than itself.
And each story is its answer.

What, then, can I do but listen?

Left

He will put the sheep on his right and the goats on his left . . .
He will say to those on his left, "Depart from me, you who are
cursed . . . for I was hungry and you gave me nothing to eat,
I was thirsty and you gave me nothing to drink."

—MATTHEW 25:41–42

In Glori's story, there are two sets of dogs: Rwandan and European.

At the start of the killing, L'Ecole Technique Officielle was a haven for whites and Rwandans, a refuge for Europeans and Tutsi together.

Outside the walls were machetes and corpses. Inside were U.N. soldiers—*peacekeepers*—with guns.

The soldiers refused to stop the killing, refused to shoot to protect the living, the soon-to-be-dead. Fearing disease, they shot instead the Rwandan dogs feeding on the bodies outside the gates.

The patient killers looked on, in peace.

This is one reason Glori hates dogs.

Then trucks came for the waiting whites—expats, business owners, priests; left behind the black Rwandans—women, children, men.

No room on those trucks for babies with black skin, Glori concludes. *The whites didn't want their dogs to be killed, so they took them along.*

They left the Tutsi children. They saved their dogs instead.

She says this with a rage so pure I know I am looking into the face of God.

Pink

Whole family killed by Hutu, buried
God knows where,
and she writes the story, dry-eyed,

until she comes to a detail—pink.

Roses in their yard,
pillow on her bed,
sandals on her little sisters' feet,

her favorite blouse—pink—
a gift from her grandmother
the day she turned twelve.

On that day,
her mother made sweets.
Her father gave her
a notebook and pen.

They wanted her
to be a teacher;
she wanted to be a nurse.

They have never seen her teach.
And she has never had
another pink blouse.

In the palette of her life
there is no pink now.

Except each April,
when the blossoms burst

along the schoolyard walls,
petals littering the ground.

She has never seen a pink
so fierce,

but for the convicts' coveralls
that blaze the hillsides of Butare.

Confession

Alphonse, the Hutu house-help who saved the family, delivering water and news each day for one hundred days, risking his life to keep a dozen people from death, fled when the RPF arrived.

—better to have killed the family in their beds—

He walked for days from Butare to Kigali, back to the parents he was born to, but they had left the city with no trace.

—better to have slaughtered the cattle—

Homeless, Alphonse slept in the slums, awoke one morning beside a dead man—not genocide, simply killed in the night. Alphonse was there when the police arrived.

—better to have burned the house to the ground—

In the years that followed, those who murdered neighbors, tortured and terrorized, maimed and robbed, faced *gacaca*. One by one, they confessed and were freed.

—better to have taken all I could carry when I left—

Ten years, fifteen, Alphonse waited in prison with no trial. His only crime: sleeping and waking in the wrong place.

Better for me, he says, *to have killed the family in their beds. Better to have slaughtered the cattle. Better to have burned the house to the ground. Better to have taken all I could carry when I left.*

To that, he says, *I could have confessed. For that, I could have gone free.*

Return to Remera

The house where they hid
is seared in her cells:

the blue gate, the number of steps
from road to door.

She can smell the rain in the yard,
feel the reach of the cassava
she climbed to peer over the wall.

Her mother planted the bushes
that bloom near the walk
—pink, yellow, white—
extravagant blossoms fat as a fist.

Fifteen years later,
with a home of her own,
she returns,

paces once more
road to door, door to garden,
garden to wall,

leaves with a cutting
to start a new plant.

She carries it, cradled, through the gate,
this bare stem—

all thorns, no rose.

Dry Bones

This is what the Sovereign Lord says: My people,
I am going to open your graves and bring you up from them;
I will bring you back to the land of Israel.

—EZEKIEL 37:12

For sixteen years
Louise has carried her family
in her heart. Without warning
a memory will intrude: a piece of cloth,
a turn of head, a bit of song.

This is a fire she must feed
to keep from going out.

Now, her parents
will have a proper burial;
their bones will be moved
from mass grave
to memorial site.
There will be a service:
remembrance, stories, prayers.

Louise says she will accompany
her parents' bones on the move—

as if anyone could know
which are the remains
of her family; as if, at the new site,
anyone could keep track.

But Louise has great faith:
God and her parents will know.
The reburial will take three days.

As she walks with her parents
across the valley of dry bones,
will flesh and blood once more
take shape in her mind?

She does not remember
her mother's hands, her father's voice,
their smiles, their eyes.

She cannot forgive them for dying.

She does not want to know
who the murderers were,
has no wish for restitution.
Who can restore what was taken?

She does not know how to say
that her once-hollow self has grown strong,

that her only wish now is for memory to rest,
for ash to be ash,
so at last she can let burn down

the fire she has tended all these years.

SANCTUS

At the Hotel Bar

the journalist in flip-flops
is typing up his notes.

Now he eats fried chips,
now he drinks draft Primus as he works.

Now he turns from the keyboard,
his hands over his face.

His sobs wrack the room.

Watching a Man Cut the Grass

My first sight
of a machete

at work: blue-black
blade, honed

silver edge, it slices
even and clean,

catches red
dirt, flings it

sharp against my thigh.

Lifelines

Two men in cobalt coveralls
unload metal milk cans
from an open truck

—ten gallon tins,
a handle on each side.

My Dutch grandfather
drove Minnesota gravel roads
a century ago, collecting milk

from farmers on his route
in those same tins.

His overalls were denim-striped.
At night he smelled of pipe tobacco,
Holsteins, hay, black earth.

Tins, filled and emptied—

milk is life.
Sun and rain are life.
Hard work and soil, black or red,

the hands that grip the handle,
the back and arms that lift—

how my grandfather loved
what he did each day, and how, at night,
he slept.

Before Memorial Week: April 5, 2009

Today, at sunset—

backlit above the horizon,
a thundercloud rises, almost holy.

Fifteen years ago
there would have been days

like this: hot sun,
cool shade as clouds

rolled over the hills. The vines
would have bloomed

in orange and crimson fury.
There would have been morning birds

and birdsong, children
and music, drums speaking

into the night—the late smells
of charcoal and cigarettes.

Men would have sat in doorways
as now, greeting neighbors,

sharing beer, while mothers
tucked babies into bed.

Later still, couples would have
made love, conceived

the future with hope, lying
silent after, listening

to distant thunder—awaiting,
as I do now, the coming storm.

Poolside after Dark

The palms are still,
cascades of fronds

unmoving and unmoved.
The surface of the pool is glass.

A waiter brings avocado on china,
a carafe of red wine.

>Once, Tutsi haunted this pool
>drawing water for drinking,
>for cooking, for bathing.
>*Amazi* was life.

>Once, palm fronds were stripped,
>tree branches cut,
>brush became fire.
>*Umuriro* was life.

>Once, red wine bought favors
>and white skin meant safety—
>night offered cover,
>not peace.

In this place—
the sharp thorns

of history, the blood-
stain of voices.

In this place—
the blossoms of loss.

Testimony

The songbird in the crown
of the princess palm
is singing so loudly her liquid
notes lift over the children in the yard,
the chatter on the deck, the music
that is never turned off. Whether
from love or fear,
her voice

vaults clear and far—
persistent and undeterred. She lands
on the open bar, beside
a man drinking alone. Such iridescent
wings—she is a flower with feathers,
song with a beating
heart. The man looks,
looks away.

Meeting François in Heaven

Do you want to start with soup?
François asks, though he already knows.

Here in Heaven, I always eat
the same thing, so of course I will have

the peanut squash soup.
We have rehearsed

this not-knowing, our talk
limited to soup, curry,

a cup of black coffee
and *No thank you* to dessert.

François is a survivor: a dark dent
above his ear, where no hair grows—

the place where death
was printed on his skull

and then erased. I want to trace it
with my finger: smooth it

like a sculptor. Caress it like a healer.
Ease it, like a mother.

Samuel and the Boys

Eight street boys appeared
at Samuel's door.
They chose names for themselves,
asked for food, a place to sleep,
and money for school.

Three times they were sent away
before Samuel took them in.

Now they tell me their lives
as Samuel looks on:

turns of family fortune,
cruel relatives,
beatings, sickness, hunger,
and brushes with death.

Samuel, they say,
has given them food, clothes, shelter—
haircuts and school.

They tell me
how things have changed:
milk and maize,
mattresses on the floor,
tea for breakfast, and books.

They are happy, they say,
to have such a normal life.

But it is not their happiness,
or their stories I love;

it is the way the boys tell them,
practiced edges worn smooth,

and the way Samuel
watches them as they speak—
proud as any of the fathers
they no longer have.

Gorilla Family *Amahoro*

The scar on the tracker's cheek
extends his smile lopsidedly—or perhaps
creates the illusion of a smile.

It is not his job to help me. He is
for the gorillas, lives with the group *Amahoro*
in the mountains of Volcanoes Park.

But with his left hand he takes mine,
guides me up the slippery path, across stinging
nettles, over young bamboo

and underbrush to where the silverback
has stopped to eat, to the gathering
of juveniles, females, and babies.

This is the family he knows,
and he speaks to them in guttural
growls, which they return.

In his right hand, he wields a *panga*
with skill, a lifetime of practice, expertly slicing
through vines and vegetation

to clear my way. A tool of destruction
or a means of escape? I feel safe in the hands
of the man whose language

I cannot understand. I have nothing
to offer in return but a smile
and a word—the name given the family

surrounding us, here in this far corner
of Rwanda: *Amahoro. Peace*—a nation's wish
borne on a silvered back.

Umuganda

No dust rises from the red dirt roads.
No lines of people cross the bridge.
No trucks spew black smoke up the hills.

The petrol station is closed—
all doors locked, security bars in place.

Weddings wait, ceremonies are delayed.

The children selling phone cards,
magazines, and maps of Africa
are gone—

the quiet fountain
in the City Centre roundabout
is ringed by spokes of silent streets.

No shouts. No horns.

No soul in sight—
it's like the Rapture,
every driver, seller, beggar taken up.

More dazed by this loud silence
than the teeming chaos
I have come to know,

I cannot stand the heated stillness,
cannot bear to walk, alone,
these emptied, burning streets.

Reparations

Each day, distant hills dissolve
under gathering clouds,
eucalyptus tops blur, the world
becomes small and near.

Each day, far-off thunder
and shifting winds
stir the magpies to flight.
Each day, torrents of rain.

The ferns grow regal here,
the rivers fill, flowers bloom
purple, yellow, fuchsia,
and pink.

   At dawn: a bright bird, fallen
   by the side of the walk, so small
   I could have held it in my palm—
   perfect red feathers, perfect black beak.

   At dusk: a rainbow, bent
   over trumpet trees, charcoal fires—
   prayers of a vespered tongue
   entreating the stars.

Now the ochre dust settles,
the leaves and fronds gleam.
The mantled moon breaks
through prisms of night.

Rwanda Stands up for Haiti: January 2010

because they know that black skin
      makes pain invisible and history mute;

because they share the language of the master;

because they know the white world hungers
      for brown babies, and their children
      are stolen in the name of better lives,
      and sometimes they have to let them go;

because they, too, have posted photos
      of the missing, begged
      to know who is still alive,
      whose bodies have been found;

because they have collected bones
      that bear no names;

because they know that tragedy
      brings the world to your door
      —all amnesia, apology, good will—
      long after the lights have gone out;

because they have had to say *thank you*
      for help that was no help,
      too little, too late;

because there is never enough medicine,
      clean water or food,
      and the poorest always do without;

because they have been shaken;

because they are tired of saying *yes*
        when they can't afford to say *no*;

because they have risen from ashes and dust;

because they know that song is prayer and prayer
        is their only hope;

because on the rubble of their dreams
        the moon shines,
        the earth turns,
        and the nights and the days go on.

Language Lessons

Only one thing remained reachable,
close and secure amid all losses: language.
—PAUL CELAN

Language is power, forming
clouds over each speaker's head—
rain blessing, the mother-tongue
eloquence we are born into,
our first inheritance and gift.

. . .

The colonizers brought their own
words, worn smooth: cushioned
consonants, languorous vowels,
seduction shaping the sounds—
the language of love.

. . .

I don't like to hear
how the French
armed the *génocidaires*,
trained them to fight,
lured out those in hiding,
promising *safe now*
as killers approached.
These roots of black bloodshed
are white, polished blades
hidden among the words.

. . .

Abel's brother is bleeding to death
with a thousand others in a church.
He takes Abel's hand, places it

on his open wound. *Rub the blood*
on yourself, he says. *Lie down.*
They will think you are dead.
Abel listens and lives.

     • • •

Emery says the names of those
who died are a song; the names of
those who saved others are a poem.
Remember the names, he says.

     • • •

On display in Kigali—
a piece of the moon,
taken from the Sea of Tranquility,
which is no sea at all.
The fragment, a gift from the U.S.,
bears this note: *One World—One Peace.*

     • • •

The guard at the hotel door
teaches me words in his world,
a map drawn with his own hand
to help me find my way:
hello, goodbye, good morning,
good evening, thank you, tomorrow,
how are you, I am fine, and *umbrella;*
offers no words for *genocide, machete,*
or *death.*

     • • •

Mukundwa, whose name means *Beloved*,
marries Hakizimana, *God saves*.
They are survivors. But
who will speak for the fathers now?
How can their clans unite,
form ties across family lines?
They have never kissed.
In a church of witnesses
his fingertips roll up her veil,
revealing to all the face of love.
At night, she cannot stop
her tears. Over and over her heart
recites the names of her dead.

· · ·

Behind rows of microphones,
the American on stage cannot say
genocide. We have every reason to believe,
she says instead, *that acts of genocide
have occurred.* How many 'acts of genocide'
does it take to make genocide?
*There are formulations that we are using
that we are trying to be consistent in our use of . . .
I don't have an absolute categorical description
against something, but I have the definitions,
I have a phraseology which . . .*
In the time it takes
to speak these non-words—

throw a grenade into a church,
set a school on fire,
toss a toddler down a latrine.

.   .   .

During the hundred days there was only
the sound of death. What else
could be said? Every breath
was a prayer. Even the birds
were silent. Even the stars, mute.

.   .   .

Ernest tells of one who murdered
children and ever after could not escape
the voices of children in his head. Ernest
tells of another who murdered his own
friend, buried him in a pit. The victim's voice
would not be stilled. The killer dug up the body,
walked around with the skull, talking back.

.   .   .

Language is the last thing that we have.
Bitter on our tongues, it remains.

BENEDICTUS

Milkfugue

Milk is the gift of life. May God make milk for you.
Living on milk from cattle they do not kill, Tutsi are lean
and long of limb. There is milk in their mouths, milk
in their veins, the land flowing with milk—may God make milk
for you. May God make blood for you: a pact cut under the navel—
covenant consumed, a belly of blood. Blood in their mouths

and veins; milk in their veins and mouths—they are lean
and long of limb. Blood is the gift of life. May God make milk
and blood: past and future wed, from dowry cow
to milk shared over bloody morning-after sheets. Milk
for the children, blood for the elders—covenant consummated,
a belly of milk. May God make milk for you.

Milk is the gift of death. When Tutsi royals must be killed,
no blood, only milk—and they drink to their death. May God
make death for you. There is milk in the cup; there is death
in the cup. They are lean and they drink; milk is death
and they drink. The White Fathers bring their own cup
and promise—on altars, doorposts—a land flowing with milk

and a cup of blood. *Drink ye all of it.* Covenant completed,
a belly of blood: blood is the gift of death, and they drink.
In *Mata*—the month of milk—long limbs are cut until death
is all there is to drink, every stream–river–well running red.
Tutsi cattle are bled, Tutsi elders are bled, Tutsi children
are dead, every red river running—and they drink and they drink.

Blood in the water, blood in the cup, the promised land
flowing and they drink and they drink. May God make milk
for you, may God make blood for you. Milk is life is death

is blood in the cup. Every stream–river–well running red and they drink. This is blood and they drink; milk is death and they drink. They drink and they drink—all of it.

NOTES ON THE POEMS

"Genesis: The Source of the Nile," page 3

mwami: king

umurwa mukuru: capital city

John Hanning Speke was a British explorer in East Africa. From 1858 until 1863 he searched for the source of the White Nile. He believed he had located the river's origin in the great lake he named "Victoria."

In 1898, the German explorer Richard Kandt concluded that a stream feeding into Rwanda's Nyabarongo River was the true source of the Nile. Kandt went on to become the first European resident of Rwanda, establishing his administrative center in Kigali.

In the transcript of an inflammatory anti-Tutsi speech on November 22, 1992, Léon Mugesera made the claim that "Tutsi's home is in Ethiopia, but we are going to find them a shortcut, namely the Nyabarongo River."

"Six Seconds," page 11

gukora akazi: do the work

kujya ku kazi: going to work

"Genocide Site 1: Nyamata Church," page 15

Nyamata is a town situated in the Bugesera District of Rwanda about thirty-five kilometers south of Kigali. Nyamata and the surrounding area comprise one of the regions most devastated in 1994. The Catholic Church in Nyamata was the site of the murder of more than ten thousand individuals (some believe the number is closer to twenty-five thousand to thirty thousand). Tutsi—along with Hutu who opposed the genocide, who were perceived as Tutsi, or who were thought to be sympathetic to Tutsi—were killed. The exact number of victims at any given location is difficult to determine due to shifts in the boundaries for what constitutes a site (a church, an adjacent school, a walled compound in which the buildings are located, the village area that surrounds the site), the inclusion of children too young to be on the official "rolls," as well as the relocation of victims' remains. In particular, this genocide site commemorates the brutal treatment of women during the genocide, including rape and the resulting extension of genocide through the spread of HIV.

"Genocide Site 2: Ntarama Church," page 16

Ntarama is a church located about thirty kilometers south of Kigali in the Bugesera District. Ntarama was the site of the murder of five thousand Tutsi and Hutu associated with Tutsi. The church and its contents now comprise a genocide memorial. When I visited the site in 2006, the memorial still contained bodies where they had fallen during the attack on the church. There were sorting rooms in the buildings around the sanctuary, where human remains and artifacts were being organized.

"Eucharist," page 18

There are many shocking examples where the Church and church personnel (priests, nuns, pastors) were complicit in genocide; there are also many stories that offer instances of grace—church workers who displayed courage and kindness, hiding, protecting, and even giving their lives to defend potential victims.

"Church at Nyange," page 21

Interahamwe translates literally to "those who stand/work/fight together." It refers to a paramilitary organization formed by groups of young Hutu males who were trained to massacre and who served as civilian death squads, carrying out particularly brutal attacks against Tutsi and Hutu associated with Tutsi.

The church at Nyange no longer exists, though the site itself is a genocide memorial containing numerous mass graves. The outline of the church's foundation can still be seen in the dirt, and the entire area is littered with broken bricks.

Father Athanase Seromba, the vicar of the parish, was convicted by the International Criminal Tribunal for Rwanda (ICTR) for having ordered and participated in the crimes at Nyange.

"Rift," page 26

umuzungu: white person

"The Lives of Others," page 28

murakoze: thank you

"Left," page 30

L'Ecole Technique Officielle is a secondary school in Kigali where Belgian United Nations troops abandoned more than 2,500 Tutsi to be slaughtered by machete-wielding killers. The U.N. soldiers—termed "peacekeepers"—insisted, "We have no mandate to intervene."

"Pink," page 31

Prisoners accused or convicted of genocide are held in prison, where they wear bright pink coveralls. They are often seen on the Rwandan hillsides, working in the prison fields.

"Confession," page 33

The Rwandan Patriotic Front (RPF, also Rwandese Patriotic Front) was formed in 1987 by the Tutsi (and some Hutu) refugee diaspora, many of whom had fled the country during previous periods of ethnic persecution. During the 1994 genocide, the RPF entered Rwanda, rescuing many Tutsi in hiding and under attack, and eventually defeated the army and seized control of the country to end the hundred days of genocide. For an excellent (brief) account of the history of the RPF, the Rwandan diaspora, and the 1994 genocide, see "Rwanda: Walking the Road to Genocide" by Gerald Caplan in *The Media and the Rwanda Genocide*, edited by Allan Thompson.

In the years following genocide, the Rwandan legal system was completely given over to bringing crimes of genocide to justice. As a result, progress on other cases was significantly delayed. In addition to the formal legal system, the country experimented with *gacaca* (pronounced ga-CHA-cha). Translated roughly into English, *gacaca* means "justice on the grass," and refers to the cut grass (or *umucaca*) that served as the traditional gathering place for elders to sit to judge a trial within the community. Until its work concluded in 2012, *gacaca* court was part of a community justice system responsible for bringing to trial those accused of genocide. It was intended to make possible justice and reconciliation in post-genocide Rwanda, avoiding what would have amounted to centuries of trials had the cases been tried through conventional legal means. In *gacaca*, the defendant was accused and brought to public trial, where survivors and victims' families could confront the accused, after which the accused either confessed to his or her crimes or maintained innocence. The court then reached a verdict and determined an appropriate punishment or means of restitution. For more information on *gacaca*, see the documentary films on post-genocide Rwanda produced and directed by Anne Aghion.

"Dry Bones," page 35

In Rwanda, a period of mourning follows the funeral, during which time a fire is kept burning.

"At the Hotel Bar," page 39

The journalist at the bar is former *New York Times* reporter Stephen Kinzer, who was working on his book *A Thousand Hills: Rwanda's Rebirth and the Man Who Dreamed It*—the story of the rebuilding of post-genocide Rwanda as told through the life and words of President Paul Kagame. In his book, Kinzer relates the first-person testimonies of many survivors of genocide. A good while after I wrote this poem, I discovered that in his book, Kinzer himself mentions this exact episode at the hotel bar (317).

"Lifelines," page 41

Because of the important role milk plays in historical and contemporary Rwanda, there are several words used to describe milk containers, each based on its particular function. *Igicuba* is the container used for collecting milk in the process of milking; *icyansi* is the container for storing milk; and *inkongoro* is the container used for serving and drinking milk. In this poem, the metal tins that are being transported would be considered *icyansi*.

"Poolside after Dark," page 44

amazi: water
umuriro: fire

The pool in this poem is part of the Hôtel des Mille Collines, a large European-style hotel in Kigali. The hotel became famous as the building in which more than twelve hundred people took refuge during the genocide. The story of the hotel was used as the basis for *Hotel Rwanda*, a Western film that has garnered much acclaim, as well as much criticism for its Hollywood portrayal of the genocide and its depiction of the hotel manager, Paul Rusesabagina, as a Hollywood-style hero.

"Meeting François in Heaven," page 46

Heaven is a Western-style restaurant in Kigali that employs local orphans and vulnerable youth, providing them with salaries and health care in line with international standards.

"Gorilla Family Amahoro," page 49

panga: machete

Amahoro, which means "peace," is the name of a group of seventeen mountain gorillas normally found on the slopes of Mt. Bisoke in the Volcanoes National Park (PNV), an area in northwestern Rwanda that provides a protected haven for them and that was home to the renowned primatologist, Dian Fossey. The baby gorillas are named each year by the people of Rwanda in a ceremony known as *Kwita Izina*.

"Umuganda," *page 51*

Umuganda, meaning "contribution," has existed in Rwanda since precolonial times, when individuals would work communally, without pay, for the common good. In its contemporary form, the last Saturday of the month is declared *Umuganda*. On this day, from 7 A.M. to noon, every able-bodied person over the age of eighteen is required to work for the community on a project determined each month by the neighborhood or village in which he or she resides—cleaning roadsides, planting trees, repairing or expanding schools, and so on. With a few exceptions (e.g. people who work in health care, Adventists who worship on Saturday), anyone who does not participate or is caught conducting business during *Umuganda* is subject to fines.

"Rwanda Stands up for Haiti: January 2010," *page 53*

After the 2010 earthquake in Haiti, organizations in Kigali held a fundraising benefit to send support to victims of the disaster.

"Language Lessons," *page 55*

The American on stage is State Department press spokesperson Christine Shelley. In a now-infamous press conference on June 10, 1994, she held firm to the official U.S. position of avoiding use of the word "genocide" to describe events in Rwanda. When the reporter pressed to know "how many acts of genocide does it take to make genocide?" Shelley was unable to provide a coherent response.

"Milkfugue," *page 61*

Mata: April, literally translates as "milk"
The White Fathers: a Catholic missionary order

This poem borrows considerably from Paul Celan's poem "*Todesfuge*" ("Deathfugue")—written in response to the Holocaust—which uses as one of its repeated phrases: "Black milk of daybreak we drink it at evening / we drink it at midday and morning we drink it at night / we drink and we drink."

"Milkfugue" begins with and builds on the often-cited "fact" (which may at best be only partially accurate) that in precolonial times, Tutsi survived on a liquid diet, relying almost exclusively on milk, honey, and banana beer. Whether factually true or not, it is indisputable that milk was and remains a staple in Rwandan diets, and that by virtue of their ownership of cattle, Tutsi in the past had greater access to milk than did their Hutu counterparts. In precolonial times, this resulted in (or was imagined to result in) an often-differing physiognomy: Tutsi were taller and thinner, while Hutu (whose diets contained more starch and grain) were shorter and stockier. During colonial times, Europeans perpetuated these real-or-imagined differences, turning what may have been the results of class and/or dietary differences into markers of ethnicity. In modern times—with intermarriage, migration, and more varied diets— little of this distinction holds true (if it ever did), but during genocide it was nevertheless the case that individuals were "identified" at roadblocks and in mass murders by their physical shape, as well as by their identity cards. Thus, in the absence of personal familial knowledge, tall and thin Rwandans were often assumed to be Tutsi and killed, while short and stocky Rwandans were assumed to be Hutu and let live.

In the poem, the blood pacts (which involved the drinking of blood) were a sign of lifelong loyalty between clans or between friends— including friendships between Hutu and Tutsi. (See L. Fujii, *Killing Neighbors*, 63.)

At a wedding, *gutwikurura* is a milk ceremony that takes place in the bedroom of the bride and groom after the marriage has been consummated, before the bride returns to take her place in the outside world. In *gutwikurura*, elder women give milk to the bride and groom, and the bride and groom give milk to the young children. This exchange seals the union and signifies a future of prosperity and fertility for the couple.

The story of the milk poisoning of the *mwami* (king) and/or the queen mother (the mother of the ruling *mwami*) was told to me by a guide at the Museum of Rwandan Ancient History in Nyanza. He explained that to avoid trouble, the ruling *mwami* and queen mother were required to die at the same time, so that the transfer of power to a new *mwami* and queen mother would be complete. In his detailed telling, he described how after the death of one, the surviving royal was forced to drink milk until he or she also died. This allowed the transfer of power to take place without the shedding of any blood. Thus, under these circumstances, the drinking of milk led directly to death.

EPILOGUE: WRITER AS WITNESS

The facts of this world seen clearly
are seen through tears;
why tell me then
there is something wrong with my eyes?

To see clearly and without flinching,
without turning away,
this is agony
. . . .
Witness is what you must bear.

—MARGARET ATWOOD, FROM "NOTES TOWARDS
A POEM THAT CAN NEVER BE WRITTEN"

The poems in this collection were written across several years and many visits. Originally, I traveled to Rwanda to plan, with Rwandan and American colleagues, a workshop that would use narrative writing to facilitate healing among survivors of the 1994 genocide of the Tutsi. The writing-for-healing project allowed me to return to Rwanda to conduct the workshops and train facilitators, and later to present the work at an international conference in Kigali. When my role in the project ended, I made several more trips to Rwanda to focus on writing poetry of my own.

One of the goals stated by the workshop participants was that through their writings the world would hear voices and stories from Rwanda and would know what had happened there in 1994. They believed that recounting what they had witnessed would lend heft to the often-repeated but seldom-heeded mantra concerning genocides worldwide: "Never again." They believed their stories could make a difference. They had to believe it.

The poems in this collection tell a story of a different sort—my story as a writer, trying to convey what I was learning in and about Rwanda. I, too, want to believe that stories, poems, words can make a difference.

To understand how the poems in this collection came to be, it is necessary to understand the context from which they grew. This, then, is an account of that process, from the inception of the writing-for-healing project; through many visits to connect, listen, collect, and write; culminating in my return to Rwanda—poems in hand—to share my work.

Using Writing to Facilitate Healing

In 2006, I made my first visit to Rwanda. It was actually my first visit to Africa—a continent that seemed impossibly distant from the world in which I had grown up. Raised in a small Dutch Calvinist farming community in the rural United States, I knew only bits and pieces about Africa, primarily from the slideshows of missionaries who came through our town, talking about the work they were doing and generating support. I doubt I had heard of Rwanda before the 1994 genocide, and even then, when news clips thrust Rwanda into my consciousness, I still was not sure where to find it on a map, or how to understand the difference between the two main groups that to me sounded so much alike.

Then, more than a decade after the genocide, I was approached after a poetry reading by an acquaintance, Ken Bialek. Ken had just returned from Rwanda. While there, he had spent time with Rose Mukankaka and Glorieuse Uwizeye, a mother-and-daughter team who ran Association Mwana Ukundwa (AMU),[1] an organization that by then had been responsible for the care of nearly two thousand orphans of genocide. Rose and Glori explained to Ken that they were meeting the physical, educational, vocational, and spiritual needs of the orphans. But, they said, no one was attending to the orphans' psychological needs.

Ken and I talked about the healing aspects of writing. He asked if I might wish to explore such possibilities in a project in Rwanda. And so, in 2006, I made my first trip to Kigali to meet with Rose and Glori and discuss how writing might be used for psychological healing of post-traumatic stress among survivors of the genocide.

Rose, Glori, Ken, and I together developed a plan to train Rwandan facilitators in a writing-for-healing process. We decided to work with university-aged survivors who would help shape, then participate in the writing workshop. We hoped that these participants would eventually facilitate similar workshops in the communities in which they lived, studied, and worked.

Ken and I returned to Michigan with the beginnings of a plan. In the months that followed, we brought together a group consisting of local health professionals, psychiatrists, Africanists, and scholars to help us brainstorm a future for the work. Glori joined us from Kigali, and together we laid out a rationale and tentative format for the first round of workshops using writing to facilitate healing, which would be offered in 2007.

The rationale for using writing for healing is that, by definition, traumatic memories are characterized as being disorganized and incomplete. They often surface and resurface in ways that are unexpected and that cannot be controlled. Part of their extreme power is that they have little or no narrative content, existing primarily as fragments, feelings, and physical sensations that occur without warning and at unexpected times.

Therapeutic writing—that is, narrative writing that systematically follows a particular format—has been proven effective in reducing the effects of PTSD and improving mental health because it allows an individual to organize traumatic memory by converting images and emotions into words and narrative text.[2] Deliberately revisiting the trauma through writing allows the individual to control the timing of the emotional response and give order and structure to what otherwise is chaotic and out of control. As writers learn that they can move into and back out of painful memories, they begin to associate feelings of control over previously intolerable and unmanageable emotions.

With this sense of the healing potential of therapeutic writing, we returned to Kigali in November 2007. The Michigan group had expanded to include two physicians: a psychiatrist, Tatyana Sigal, and a pediatrician, Yakov Sigal. We had a general plan for the work: a week-long workshop made up of writing sessions, daily debriefing, and a discussion at the end of the week devoted to imagining a future for the work. The young people would participate in the workshop, but they would also be co-planners and would be training as facilitators to do this work in the future with other groups.

The overall design for the workshop was created based on our personal and professional experience and research. We wanted to combine a process writing approach (the format) with a therapeutic writing model (the content).³ However, although we had an idea for the general framework, it was important for us to involve the participants/facilitators in the planning as well—to hear what they needed and how they could imagine writing together in the current workshop setting as well as with future groups. Therefore, the entire group spent the first day getting to know one another, discussing possible workshop formats, and talking about our desires and intentions for the work.

The meetings were held at the Kigali Genocide Memorial Centre, located in the heart of Kigali on a hill looking overlooking the city. Constructed ten years after the genocide, the Kigali Genocide Memorial Centre marks a site where over 250,000 victims of genocide are buried in mass graves. The building is surrounded by gardens, burial vaults, and walls containing the names of victims who have been identified and are buried there. We met in a room of the on-site conference facility and took our meals together in the canteen.

Along with the four individuals from Michigan, the group consisted of six young people from Rwanda, as well as Rose and another senior Rwandan colleague (both of whom participated only in the agenda-setting on the first and last days). The young people ranged in age from twenty-five to thirty-two, meaning they had been between twelve to nineteen years old at the time of genocide. All had lost extended and/or immediate family members in the genocide, and several were orphans of genocide. Because their jobs and training put them in environments in which they had close contact with youth who had survived (or were the children of survivors), all had expressed a wish to use the skills learned in the workshop to work with children and young people in their various contexts. Individuals of this age, they said, often had no one to talk to about the genocide and were left to figure things out on their own; as a result, they frequently misunderstood facts about the genocide (both the history and what had taken place), and its reverberations through their lives were powerful and confusing.

All of the participants were highly literate—reading, writing, and speaking both in Kinyarwanda and in French, which at the time were the national languages of Rwanda. Most were also fluent in spoken English, and a few were competent (though not entirely comfortable) using written English. At times, those members of the group who were more confident working in English than the others would serve as translators. All the participants wrote in Kinyarwanda, and some of the discussion on both the first and the last days of the workshop focused on issues of language and translation.

As we talked about possibilities for the workshop, the participants vacillated between focusing on the therapeutic value of the writing process and on the therapeutic value of the written products. The young people were clear that although the process might have healing properties, they also wanted their written products to find a place in the world. Their goals were many: to document for the future their own experiences and testimonies, to use their writing to educate the children of Rwanda, and to have their words reach an audience beyond the boundaries of the country. It was clear from our conversations that they did not imagine our time together to be an end in itself. Rather, this was for them a far-reaching and ongoing enterprise, creating historical documents and curriculum within Rwanda, and letting the wider world know what had taken place and what they had experienced.

As participants engaged in the therapeutic process of the workshop, they began to experience the potential for using writing to facilitate healing. They found that the brainstorming process allowed them to access memories they had thought long forgotten, and that by focusing on the three stages (life before, during, and after genocide), they were able to return through memory to happier times in the period before genocide—something most of them said they had not done in the past. One participant explained during one of our debriefing sessions, "I was happy when I was writing [about the time before genocide] because I felt like I was back there and was with my family;" another added, "The time for writing was too short. I want to think about it when I have enough time. I want to be as happy as I was during this writing."

Participants also found that writing about genocide helped them recognize the emotions that had overwhelmed them at the time the genocide was taking place. One participant described his state of mind during the genocide in this way: "Two days after [the genocide began] I fell into dreaming. I was in a dream. . . . I was seeing fighting, dead people, people stealing in the houses of dead people. Even when I was rescued I was still dreaming. It's as if I was deep in the ocean. In 1999, I realized genocide took place." The value of writing, one of them concluded, is that it encourages people to begin to come to terms with the reality of the genocide. "Many people *still* don't want to think genocide happened," the participant said. "If someone is writing, they have to acknowledge things. They *have* to recognize that things happened."

In discussing their writing about the present and future (the post-genocide stage), many of the participants focused on a sense of personal pride in the lives they had created and the things they had done in the years following the genocide. As one participant put it, "Doing this, I realized I had made good things since genocide." Another participant explained, "I passed the national exam to go to high school. I have some independence now—I can buy groceries for myself. I have money I can lend to others. I'm a student at the university." One young woman took a long view across the many years since the genocide. She said, "After genocide, I thought I had no life because I had no parents. But that wasn't true. Other families have taken the place of my parents and do what parents do. I have other family members, even if they're not direct blood relatives." One young man, however, questioned whether there was anything positive to write about in Rwanda, post-genocide. He said, "It wasn't easy for me to write something after genocide. Though after genocide I have done many things—I survived as a soldier, I graduated, I helped other survivors and orphans. I participated in many things. I tried to write about good things, but bad things still came."[4]

When we disbanded, the participants had many tools for moving forward in their writing and many ideas for using the writing-for-healing model in their own contexts. They also had a sense that this sort of writing was of value to survivors. As one of the young men observed at the close of the workshops, "To ask someone to write is to ask them to fight. To ask someone to write is to ask them to fight for life."

Results of the Writing-for-Healing Project

A year and a half later, in April 2009, the Michigan group returned to Rwanda to present early versions of the writing-for-healing project at the International Symposium on the Genocide against Tutsi, held on the fifteenth anniversary of the genocide. Two of the workshop participants were coauthors of the presentation. Before we prepared a conclusion for our talk, we met with each of the participants individually to discuss the results of the writing-for-healing workshop from the vantage point of eighteen months and to learn what the participants had done with their narratives and with the writing-for-healing model.

Our conversations[5] revealed that over the months since the workshop, several participants had continued working on their narratives. Two had completed the writing of their stories and said that it had been the workshop model that had prompted them to embark on this telling, since it was the first time they had had access to strategies and structures that allowed them to understand or to tell "the whole story." The writing, several participants said, allowed them to say things they had never said before (and that some had not spoken of since). Participants related with pride the courage it required for them to initiate this sort of self-healing, trusting that on the other side of the painful negative memories would be some positive result. They affirmed the structure and content of the workshop format—several mentioned the "release" they had found in acknowledging, through writing, the emotions they had experienced during the genocide. One participant explained, "During brainstorming in the genocide section, I wrote about emotions I'd denied. When genocide happened, when they told me that my parents had died, I did not feel much emotion. Now, thinking and writing and crying about not having a father and mother—emotion emerged and I could retrieve it." Another explained, "Pre-genocide, genocide, post-genocide. It's good to remember them separately. Then you can resume your own life in an understanding manner."

For many, a focus on early years brought back happy memories that continued to provide them with comfort, and looking at the progress they had made in the time since genocide was positive as well. As one participant said, "Until the writing, I only thought of my history as sad. It was important to have a chance to write about positive experiences of my childhood and positive parts of my life post-genocide." Another stated, "Prior to the workshop, I didn't even like myself. Life was very dark. Now I feel much better. When I wrote about the present time, I understood that life goes on, families gather, there is hope for the future."

At the Symposium, we presented the work to a large audience of Rwandan and international scholars working on or in Rwanda. Just before our presentation, the prime minister was a respondent to another panel in which he spoke of the historical and literary necessity of having survivors not only tell their stories but—for the sake of history and art—write their stories as well. For the good of the nation, he maintained, records written by survivors themselves needed to be collected. In our presentation, we were able to add that having survivors write their testimonies was also good for the survivors' psychological well-being and recovery.

This was the last of the visits I made to Rwanda as part of a team. The writing-for-healing project had been taken up by the young people who would now function as facilitators, using the model with youth and colleagues in their personal and professional environments.

In 2013, six years after the workshop had taken place, on a return trip to Rwanda I met with most of the participants one more time. The reasons for my trip were many, but one goal was to talk with the young people about their experience of the writing-for-healing workshops once again—to hear about the status of their narratives, to learn whether they had conducted (and whether they still were conducting) writing workshops of their own.

Several of the participants had continued to write: some had gone on freewriting and taking notes as memories continued to arise; some wrote in more formal ways, completing their narratives in Kinyarwanda or in English, making them public to varying degrees. One participant created a blog for genocide survivors that had to do with writing and remembering, and in 2012 wrote a memory each day for the one hundred-day genocide remembrance period from early April to mid-July. One participant used the writing-for-healing format to design questionnaires for his own research interviewing survivors; from those interviews he created two books of survivors' testimonies.

In the hands of these young people, the writing workshop format was being used with primary school children, orphans, high school students, and adults. As one of the participants explained, "I'm still working on some of the ideas we talked about. I have a passion to do it. I feel the need. I love my country, and it's for my country, and for the people, and for myself." Another stated, "This method of testifying goes beyond academic; it is healing, it is deep, it gets in the quick of the life of survivors."

In reference to her own ongoing writing, one of the young women stated that the writing-for-healing workshop marked the start of her personal remembering. In the years after the workshop, she continued to write, and plans to use the written memories to create a book someday. Until that time, the writing itself is important to her: "I had no pictures of my parents or my brothers," she explained. "Now I do. The writing helps me create a picture in my heart."

Writing and Witness

Once the Rwandan young people had taken over the writing-for-healing project, my work in Rwanda made a significant shift. My early visits had centered on planning and conducting the writing workshops. Yet throughout each of these visits, I used my own writing as a means of holding and processing my personal experiences. I wanted to put into words the charcoal cooking fires of Kigali, the birds of prey circling high over the trees, the angel tears and trumpet vines in bloom. I wanted to commit to paper the sights and smells and sounds of the city: the dogs and roosters and smoke-belching motorbikes. I wanted to recall the crimson light streaking across the sky, the dusty red roads, the stories I was learning for the first time, and the history that undergirded it all.

Writing was a way for me to give voice to my own struggles with the complexities of being a citizen of a wealthy nation, spending time in a country that had been colonized by the West and that—during the genocide—the Western world had chosen to ignore. From the start, I was surprised by the intensity of the bond I felt to the people with whom I worked and how committed I was to the project we were planning. When at the close of the first trip I boarded the plane to return home, I was surprised as well by the loss and displacement I felt. I was acutely aware of my privilege: I could leave when I wanted, return if I chose. I could go back to my life of safety and ease. But in another sense, it was clear to me that the life to which I was returning no longer existed. I had changed irrevocably, and I needed to put that transformation into words. I needed to write about my complicated re-entry into what I termed "the amnesia I call home."

Most of my early writing occurred in a notebook I carried with me everywhere I went. The notes were sketched into rough drafts of poems on a yellow legal pad during the flight that brought me home. Back in the United States, I typed up those scribblings and shared them with a few close friends—a shorthand for where I had been and what I had learned. The poems were a way to let lines and stanzas and words help me sort through my early understandings and reflect on the beginnings of the project on which we had embarked.

When I returned to Rwanda in July 2007, it was for a wedding rather than for the writing-for-healing project, though of course some of that planning did take place. There were days of marriage ceremonies, all of which were rich with significance and powerful in their emotional impact. The bride was an orphan of genocide, participating now in long-standing rituals intended to form alliances between clans and family lines. The guests at the wedding were people whose histories were known to those around them, but were completely incomprehensible to me. As representatives from the families played out their various roles, I could not help but wonder about their scars—those I could see and those hidden beneath the colorful wedding finery, the stories behind the toasts and gift-giving and smiles.

I wore an *imikenyero*—a traditional wrap—that belonged to the mother of the groom. When she wrapped the bright cloth around me for the wedding, she said, "You are family now," and I was: *Tante Rouge*—the fair-skinned "auntie" placed in the shade as the Rwandan sun burned through the days. At one point I found myself in the bedroom of the couple, with the other aunties, gathered to watch the bride and groom exchange milk as a symbol of fertility and health. When all the guests left after days of celebrating, I, along with the rest of the family, remained.

I was too busy taking notes to write any poems: the symbols, the ceremonies, the stories and histories—I wanted to commit it all to memory, jotting page after page of questions and observations, impressions and fragmented lines. I wrote no poems on the next visit, either. November 2007 was the start of the writing-for-healing project, and my role was to lead the workshops, then help the group debrief and think in larger terms about how this process might work for others. Though I collected many words and ideas, there was no time for poetry; the participants' stories (shared, written) awakened me to the specificity of their experiences. While before I had been shocked by the sheer numbers of the atrocities, in the workshop setting I was coming to know individual survivor stories through sharing, talking, reading, and writing. One young man looked out the window midway through the workshops, pointing down the hill to a small house in the dense vegetation. In the attic of that house, he said, he had hidden for much of the genocide; then, when the risk became too great, he crawled by night through the field to a church that he thought would be safe. After that explanation, he very deliberately turned his chair from the window, and for the rest of the workshop sessions, chose a seat that did not offer him the window view of those hills.

It was not until my fourth trip, in April 2009, that I wrote a poem while I was actually on the ground in Rwanda. Being in Kigali in early April (the time of remembrance—a yearly commemoration) was power-ful for me as an outsider and stirred again my desire to translate emotions into words. I was highly aware that I was standing in a place that—years earlier—had been the scene of some of the most horrific events of the late-twentieth century, but that now was beautiful and tranquil, with tropical flowers and seasonal rains. I imagined this was how it might have been for Rwandans before the genocide began, how the first days of April 1994 might have unfolded in ordinary ways—the rains, the sun, the muddy roads much the same as they were now, fifteen years later.

It was good to see the young people again; their lives had moved for-ward, and they were entering a period characterized by graduations, new jobs, weddings, and babies. As well, the symposium provided a rich back-drop of politics and history that transformed my view of the genocide and shifted my thinking about the poems. I was learning first-hand about the effects of Rwanda's colonial history, the role of the West in the years and months and weeks leading up to genocide, the failure of "developed" nations to intervene even though they knew a genocide was taking place. I was moving from being a naive observer, filled with a turbulent and complex mix of emotions, into being a more informed witness to the out-come of my own country's policies. My writing was less a way to process new information; I started to see my writing as poems, and my poems as a form of social action. When I shared my stories of Rwanda back home, I realized that most people were as I had been—unaware of Rwandan history, quick to assume that the genocide was just a spontaneous eruption of violence between two African "tribes" rather than something carefully planned and executed over many years. The more I learned, the more I wanted to share, and poetry was my platform.

I started taking the poems seriously then and began reading widely about the genocide—testimonies of survivors; accounts written about the roles of the church, the media, the U.N.; works that focused on the planners, perpetrators, and victims; reports about the *gacaca* process and the Arusha tribunal courts. I needed a solid sense of the past and present, a wider backdrop against which to write.

The young people had taken over the writing-for-healing project by then, which allowed my full attention to shift to my poems. In January 2010, I received university support to return to Rwanda to work on my poetry. The writing-for-healing workshop had set the stage, and I remembered the desire the participants had had to have their stories go out into the world. I shared that desire. And though I knew I could not—nor did I wish to—speak *for* the people with whom I had worked, I also was clear that in writing about my experiences of post-genocide Rwanda, I would include my hearing of and response to some of the stories I had been told.

I spent three weeks in Rwanda, staying at a small guesthouse in Kigali. I was not part of a team; occasionally I saw some of my Rwandan friends, but for the most part I was on my own. My days developed a rhythm of reading, walking, drafting, and revising. Every dinner was a solitary affair. At one point, when I entered a restaurant where I had become a regular guest, the hostess said, "Just one?" with a knowing smile. The waiter asked, while other curious waitstaff looked on, "What is it that you are doing? Why do you always have a notebook with you while you eat?"

As the time progressed, my poems took a different quality. Instead of using writing to explore my own turbulent emotions, I began to describe what I observed of everyday life around me in Kigali—sometimes against the backdrop of history, sometimes as an end in itself. Many of my poems tried to capture this sense of dailiness—of life in and around the city. I combed through the notes I had taken, visit after visit, filling in gaps, finding the poems that waited between the lines.

I stretched my January funding to cover an additional trip in May 2010, and returned to Rwanda to draft what I expected would be the final poems for the book. As my flight landed in Kigali, I wondered about the need for the work I was doing. Looking out the window of the plane, I saw the curves of the land and the vivid squares of color and texture I had grown to love. In the seats around me were Rwandans flying home, as well as tourists and business people coming to visit what had become one of the safest and fastest-developing countries in Africa. As we touched down, I recorded in my notebook the sense I had that I, an *umuzungu*,[6] was facing backward while the rest of the country was moving on. As we stood to disembark, I was stunned to see a deep scar gouged across the back of the neck of a man a couple of rows ahead. I wrote in my journal that night: "I have never been more aware of the difficulty of witness—that is, how awful it is to look, how awful it is to look away, how little I have to say, and how important it is that I say it. The book is not about genocide, but genocide is a scar that runs the length of it, the horror I have no right to tell, yet no right to ignore."

It was the start of what emerged as a theme of the trip and of the collection as a whole: my role and responsibility as an outsider, taking in stories, sights, historical moments, and present-day events. I had come a long way from the early jottings I had used to sort my feelings on the yellow legal pad. When I revisited a genocide site that I had viewed on my first trip, I brought to the experience (and the writing that followed) not only the horror I had felt on the early visit, but also a greater knowledge of the country's complex history, the role of the Church, and the deep questions that had been growing in me in the intervening years. I recognized, on an experiential level, that it was not enough to say "never again." I was beginning to imagine my poems as a call to action. I believed my words had work to do in the world.

I started then to think of my poems as a form of "poetry of witness."[7] I was witnessing a country in the aftermath of genocide—its recovery, its enduring scars, the ongoing challenges the people faced. I was acting as a witness, putting into words what I saw and heard. I was bearing witness, holding out to potential readers my own sense of historical events, personal stories, and complicated pasts, wanting others to hear and act. And I was also being witnessed: a lone white woman with a notebook and pen.

Responses in Rwanda

In early 2013, I made one more trip to Rwanda. My purposes were many: as a workshop facilitator, I wanted to hear about the continuing results of the writing-for-healing project. As a poet, I had an additional poem I wanted to write—a complicated poem about milk that would conclude the collection, drawing from images throughout the other poems and, in tandem with the opening "Genesis: The Source of the Nile," that would describe how categories of race and ethnicity were historically constructed in Rwanda. The "milk" poem required that I learn more about the cultural history of Rwanda, and so I visited museums in Kigali and elsewhere in the country, listening to stories, reading about the *mwami* (Rwandan kings), and gathering information about colonial history and the role of milk, both in historic and present-day Rwanda. As it took shape, "Milkfugue" came to represent the full-circle route I had traveled over the years: from a writing-for-healing project for others, to writing for understanding for myself, to writing as a means of prompting readers to action; from poems that focused on my learning and coming to terms with the recent genocidal past of Rwanda, to a collection that conveyed what I had learned and how I made sense of the complicated precolonial and colonial history as I now understood it.

The real reason for my 2013 trip, though, was that I was ready to share the almost-completed poetry manuscript with my Rwandan colleagues and friends. In part, I wanted to show them that this was one more "result" of the writing-for-healing work we had done together—that their stories and experiences as Tutsi in Rwanda would go forward to an English-speaking readership, not as verbatim narratives but mixed with my own observations, my reading, and the many stories I had gathered and heard. I also needed to know if things were "factually" correct from a Rwandan standpoint and to determine whether there were any poems or parts of poems that my colleagues, as Rwandans, found problematic. As well, I needed to know whether my colleagues wished to be identified in the book (and occasionally in the poems) by their own names, or if I should provide pseudonyms, which they could really only answer after reading the manuscript and discussing what was involved.

Above all, I wanted my Rwandan colleagues to be included in what was to be the final stage of the poetic process. They had accompanied me in this work for years, both in person and as the voices that called me to write. I wanted them to accompany me in this last stage as well.

Bringing the work back to Rwanda was terrifying—by far the scariest thing I had done as a writer. And yet, the responses I received were beyond what I could have wished. My Rwandan colleagues read with care, and gently but insistently corrected my mistakes. They clarified things they were not sure I understood. They pushed against poems they found troubling or confusing.

We talked at some length about the difference between literal, factual "happening-truth" and the kind of "story-truth"[8] a writer employs by selecting specific details, focusing on particular aspects and not others, shifting and revising non-essential facts in order to make a point. My readers were quick to understand the art behind the tellings and to think in complex ways about which choices might be viewed as acceptable and which were more problematic. They were also uncompromising in their need to have the stories "told right," and I agreed—even when in one case it meant removing a poem from the collection.

Throughout the visit, my Rwandan colleagues affirmed the impulse that led me to do the writing and the importance of my return. One of the participants concluded our conversation by saying, "I think it's good that you're showing your work to genocide survivors. In your approach, the genocide survivors have a say. Sometimes, in Rwanda, someone comes with a notebook, a camera. They talk to two or three people. The next week they go home and publish something without giving it any time or checking with anyone. That's not the right way to do things. This takes time."

The last of the workshop participants with whom I shared the manuscript confirmed my sense that even twenty years later, these stories were worth putting into poems. He wrote to me, "People who visit Rwanda are stunned and amazed by the beauty of the landscape, the progress, infrastructures, people's courtesy, and this produces sometimes a distorted picture of the real genocide survivors' conditions. In my view as a survivor, the general progress and tremendous strides Rwanda as a nation has made after the genocide sometimes overshadow the special challenges survivors are still facing."

His words spoke to my own question about whether I was returning to a part of history that Rwandans wished to leave behind. There are, indeed, scars as well as unhealed wounds in Rwanda. It is often the case that certain kinds of forgetting *do* help survivors recover, and Rwanda, in particular, seems to have developed strategies to encourage individuals to move on. But not everything is forgotten. Every year in early April, the country pauses for a week to recall what for most people could never be imagined in the first place.[9] Medical personnel stand ready, as do pastors, psychiatrists, and others trained to aid individuals whose memories threaten to overwhelm them.

Thus, there is in Rwanda a highly organized means of moving forward and looking back. But for the rest of the world, it seems necessary to remember as well. Human history seems bent toward amnesia. To create an opportunity for readers to acknowledge and understand the past—and the present as well—was both a challenge and an inescapable call. Though it has been two decades since the genocide, and much has changed, it is also the case that in Rwanda this piece of history will never go away. As one of my Rwandan colleagues put it, "Two decades is not long enough to forget. A lifetime is not long enough."

Witnessing as a White Woman

Over the years that this project spans, I have been plagued by recurring questions and doubts: How do I work at the intersection of my own stories and the stories of others? Have I unintentionally spoken for others rather than for myself? What, after all, do I know about this country? And what does it mean to be a Western white woman, writing in and about Rwanda?

I have struggled throughout to articulate the relationship between my stories and the stories of others. It was never my intent to tell the stories of others as ends in themselves; rather, I wished to have them seen as a backdrop against which my own changing understanding took place.

Early on, my impulse was to see everything as irreducibly split: then or now, sad or happy, horror or beauty, wounded or healed, cursed or blessed, my stories or those of others. But the poems taught me it was all of a piece—curse and blessing woven of the same cloth, beauty and horror in the curve of each hill and the heat of each rising sun. The past and the present are inextricably intertwined. My stories are embedded in the stories of others; their stories give shape and substance to mine.

The poems represent personal discovery. They have taught me much about the world, humankind, and our capacity both for love and for cruelty. At the same time, the process of writing the poems also allowed me to learn—in a manageable way—what to me was both unmanageable and unimaginable. Stalin is reported to have said, "When one person dies, it's a tragedy, but when a million people die, it's a statistic." And in his book on the Holocaust, Timothy Snyder writes that the barbarism of mass killing is to turn people into numbers; therefore, "it is for us as humanists to turn the numbers back into people." [10] For me, it was impossible to take in numbers like eight hundred thousand killings in one hundred days, but I could understand one story or two. I could not comprehend large-scale forgiveness and reconciliation in the face of such atrocity, but I could listen to one woman's account of moving forward.

From the start, I was highly aware of the complications of being in Rwanda as a woman from a Western country and the ways white skin, class, and nationality rendered me an outsider to the culture around me and provided me power, safety, and choice. At my hotel, I had the luxury of hot running water while children around me carried yellow jugs from the streams and city wells; within sight of dirt floors and charcoal cooking fires, I had smooth sheets, a European breakfast, electric lighting, and the Internet in my room.

All around me were historical and present-day reminders of the past and of Western economic power. But the reminders of whiteness went deeper by far. At one point, early on, Glori was telling me about her experience and said, "During and after genocide, I couldn't understand why white people hated us so much, why they would leave and let us be killed, why they didn't *do* something." Of course I had no response. I wondered the same thing myself, but I now was also implicated in her wondering. And while I could not answer Glori's question, I could hold that painful query up to poetic consideration; I could present Glori's question—and my own—to a wider audience through poems.

It goes without saying that my poems are unavoidably narrow in focus and perspective, based only on what I myself have learned, experienced, and discovered. This is surely a liability, but it is also, perhaps, a strength, turning distant statistics into individuals with dust on their feet, scars on their skulls, milk tins in their hands. I have faith that stories matter, and I have faith that it is important for me to tell my story through poems, but I will also admit at the outset that the story I tell is thoroughly bounded by the limits of what I have learned and currently understand.

The poems written in and about my work in Rwanda form a specific record of my experience of a particular time. In a larger sense, though, they also chronicle the ways a white woman raised in the rural United States entered and began to understand a country and a group of people so different from what she knew. Throughout, the poems taught me the power of privilege; I recognize the ways that the happenstance of birthplace, family, status, and opportunity make it possible for me to engage with the experience of another and make it equally possible for me to stop. I can look, and I can look away. I can listen, and I can stop listening, turning my attention elsewhere.

But the poems revealed what my privilege makes impossible as well. I could not avoid being a white woman with all it conferred. I could not spend time in Rwanda without confronting and acknowledging the past—not only my personal past, but also the past of colonialism and of Western neglect and culpability in the more recent history of the country and in the lives of the individuals around me. With this knowledge came uncertainty: Do I, a white woman and academic, have a right in this context to speak? This is something I have asked often, both during my time in Rwanda and during my writing of the poems. No—as I wrote in my journal years ago, I do not have the right to speak. But at the same time, I do not have the right *not* to speak. I am stranded between "the poles of entitlement and obligation."[11] If I resist entitlement, I shirk obligation. I cannot have one without the other.

And so I have written because my silence seems to do more harm than my words. I have written because I was encouraged to write by the Rwandans I came to know. I have written because I could not keep myself from writing. Yet I know, as I write, that my whiteness is what simultaneously gives me voice and makes that voice suspect, what both legitimizes and makes illegitimate what I learned and what I wrote.

Writer as witness. I didn't know when I first agreed to be part of a project in Rwanda that it would transform my work, my writing, and my life. I went to Rwanda to explore the possibilities of using writing for healing with others; before long, I began using writing to manage my personal confusion, rage, compassion, and grief. Eventually the writing took a purpose of its own, beyond anything I could have foreseen.

I witnessed; I was a witness; I gathered the witness of others. When I spoke, I spoke as an Other, spoke with others, and occasionally spoke for others. I wove my life and words into the lives and words around me.

Carolyn Forché says that poems of witness are written in order not to forget. Margaret Atwood maintains that seeing clearly is itself an excruciating act of witness. In my experience of Rwanda, there were stories to be written and told, and they were loud and heavy stories—sometimes too loud and too heavy for my heart. But I have been compelled to hear and tell what has been entrusted to me—to testify to what I have seen and learned and felt.

Witness is, indeed, what the writer must bear.

NOTES

Prologue: A Brief History of Rwanda

1. This part of Rwandan history is in contrast with most modern African nations, whose borders, drawn by colonial powers, did not correspond to ethnic boundaries or precolonial kingdoms.
2. "The White Fathers"—a Catholic order—established missions and schools in Rwanda as early as 1903.
3. The Twa were a very small minority population in the area thought to be descendants of the earliest settlers of the region. In discussions of the ethnic history of Rwanda, the Twa are rarely mentioned due to their small numbers and the minimal role they play in ethnic conflict.
4. Throughout, I follow the Anglicized form of Kinyarwanda (the official language of Rwanda) that uses the terms "Hutu" and "Tutsi" as adjectives as well as to denote both singular and plural nouns.
5. For more on the role of the RPF before and during genocide, see Notes on the Poems, "Confession" (65).
6. For a highly detailed account of the period preceding the genocide, see *The Persecution of Rwandan Tutsi Before the 1990–1994 Genocide* by Antoine Mugesera.
7. The event for which the groundwork was being laid was described by planners as an "Apocalypse" against the Tutsi—a "final solution" to "the Tutsi problem."
8. The exact number of dead is frequently contested and has changed over time depending on recovery efforts (bones are still being discovered and identified, and the dead are still being buried and reburied), as well as on how victims are counted (for example, death as a result of rape during genocide by HIV-infected individuals is considered by many to be genocide death, and thus, even years later, the numbers continue to rise). A detailed census in July 2000 cited 951,018 victims, but estimated the death toll at over a million. Of this, 93.7 percent of the victims were killed because they were identified as Tutsi; 1 percent because they were related to, married to, or friends with Tutsi; 0.8 percent because they looked like Tutsi; and 0.8

percent because they were opponents of the Hutu regime or were hiding people from the killers (Melvern, *Conspiracy to Murder*, 252–253).

9. It is easy, in a brief overview such as this, to seem to draw clear lines between Hutu and Tutsi, genocide perpetrators and genocide victims. National memorial sites and ceremonies reinforce this binary view. However, during the genocide, these neat boundaries often were blurred: there were Tutsi who were killers, and there were Hutu who acted with courage and compassion, often at great risk to themselves and their families. More salient still, there are many examples of individuals who were both perpetrators *and* saviors, sometimes acting as killers or accomplices to killers, sometimes performing acts of heroism and rescue. And there is evidence that some members of the RPF, in stopping the genocide, killed Hutu civilians in ways that also have been viewed as ethnically motivated.

10. For a firsthand account of what was known to the West and when it was known, see *Shake Hands with the Devil*, by Lieutenant-General Roméo Dallaire. Dallaire was the Force Commander of the United Nations Assistance Mission for Rwanda (UNAMIR) during the months leading up to—and during—the genocide.

11. Andrew Wallis lays out a case for the involvement of France in the genocide of the Tutsi in his book, *Silent Accomplice: The Untold Story of France's Role in the Rwandan Genocide*.

12. In 1994, a new word, *ihahamuke*, appeared in Kinyarwanda to describe the psychological problems (post-traumatic stress and chronic grief) that were the result of genocide.

13. UNICEF estimated that more than 95,000 children were orphaned at the time of genocide. Ten years after genocide, an estimated 101,000 children were heading approximately 42,000 households, and by 2010, the number of orphans had climbed to 350,000, due to the deaths of women through the spread of HIV/AIDS by genocide rape.

14. *Gacaca* literally means "justice on the grass." Until the work of gacaca officially concluded in 2012, it served as a form of citizen-based justice that Rwanda put into place as a means to deal with the crimes of the 1994 genocide. For more information on gacaca, see Notes on the Poems, "Confession."

15. One legacy of the ICTR is that, as a result of the trials, for the first time rape

was considered to be an act of genocide, and leaders who incited genocidal violence through speech were held accountable for the actions that resulted from their words.

Epilogue: Writer as Witness

1. *Mwana ukundwa* translates to "beloved children."
2. See, for example, the research work of James W. Pennebaker.
3. In a process approach, writing occurs in multiple steps: brainstorming/freewriting, narrative writing, and revision. The therapeutic model breaks the writing content into three discrete stages: life before the trauma, the trauma itself, and life after the trauma, including hopes for the future. In the model we developed, we combined these into a three-step writing process across three stages of participant life-experiences.
4. The model we relied on assumes a "post-genocide," post-trauma period. But of course the psychological and social wounds of mass violence go on—both for the individual and for the community—long after the physical violence ends. Therefore, one aspect of this sort of work is not only to nurture hope, but also to support the ongoing work of mourning—to create a context and audience for expressions of continuing anger, fear, or grief.
5. Some discussions were conducted in English; some were conducted in French by Frank Biocca, an additional member who had joined the Michigan team.
6. *Umuzungu* translates to "white person."
7. Carolyn Forché uses the term "poetry of witness" to describe the writings of poets who have endured violence firsthand. This use is different from my use of the term to describe my own work, coming to write as a "witness" more than a decade post-genocide. In both uses of the term, though, the poems have the intent of bearing witness—of remembering, of not forgetting, of both reporting on and feeling the weight of what has gone before.
8. The terms "happening-truth" and "story-truth" are taken from the work of writer Tim O'Brien, who blends fiction and autobiography in his writings about the Vietnam War.

9. I was able to attend the yearly memorial service for the first time in 2014. I was invited to participate in the Kigali International Forum on Genocide—a gathering of legislators, policy makers, scholars, and media representatives from around the world, who came together to conduct an in-depth assessment of the legacy of the genocide, including responses to the tragedy and enduring challenges of justice, education, and reconstruction. The genocide memorial service, held in the Amahoro Stadium of Kigali, was titled Kwibuka20 and commemorated the twenty years since genocide with music, testimonies, and drama, along with speeches by President Paul Kagame and other Rwandan and world leaders. Throughout the entire remembrance week, Rwandans across the nation gathered daily in cities, in villages, and on the hills of the countryside to remember their history through stories, music, homilies, and poems.

10. Timothy Snyder. *Bloodlands: Europe Between Hitler and Stalin*, 408

11. James Dawes. *That the World May Know: Bearing Witness to Atrocity*, 24.

ADDITIONAL RESOURCES

Print

Adekunle, Julius. *Culture and Customs of Rwanda*. Westport, CT: Greenwood, 2007.

Barnett, Michael. *Eyewitness to a Genocide: The United Nations and Rwanda*. Ithaca, NY: Cornell University Press, 2002.

Benaron, Naomi. *Running the Rift: A Novel*. Chapel Hill, NC: Algonquin of Chapel Hill, 2012.

Burnet, Jennie E. "Whose Genocide? Whose Truth? Representations of Victim and Perpetrator in Rwanda." In *Genocide: Truth, Memory, and Representation*, edited by Alexander Laban Hinton and Kevin Lewis O'Neill, 80–112. Durham, NC: Duke University Press, 2009.

Burnet, Jennie E. *Genocide Lives in Us: Women, Memory, and Silence in Rwanda*. Madison, WI: The University of Wisconsin Press, 2012.

Caplan, Gerald. "Rwanda: Walking the Road to Genocide." In *The Media and the Rwanda Genocide*, edited by Allan Thompson, 20–37. Ottawa: International Development Research Centre, 2007.

Cobban, Helena. *Amnesty after Atrocity? Healing Nations after Genocide and War Crimes*. Boulder, CO: Paradigm, 2007.

Cohen, Jared. *One Hundred Days of Silence: America and the Rwanda Genocide*. Lanham, MD: Rowman & Littlefield, 2007.

Dallaire, Roméo, with Brent Beardsley. *Shake Hands with the Devil: The Failure of Humanity in Rwanda*. New York: Carroll & Graf, 2005.

Dauge-Roth, Alexandre. *Writing and Filming the Genocide of the Tutsis in Rwanda: Dismembering and Remembering Traumatic History*. Lanham, MD: Lexington Books, 2010.

Dawes, James. *That the World May Know: Bearing Witness to Atrocity*. Cambridge, MA: Harvard University Press, 2007.

de Brouwer, Anne-Marie, and Sandra Chu, eds. *The Men Who Killed Me: Rwandan Survivors of Sexual Violence*. Vancouver: Douglas and McIntyre, 2009.

Des Forges, Alison. *Leave None to Tell the Story: Genocide in Rwanda*. New York:

Human Rights Watch, 1999.

Fassin, Didier, and Richard Rechtman. *The Empire of Trauma: An Inquiry into the Condition of Victimhood*. Princeton: Princeton University Press, 2009.

Forché, Carolyn. "Introduction." *Against Forgetting: Twentieth-Century Poetry of Witness*, 27–47. New York: W.W. Norton, 1993.

Fujii, Lee Ann. *Killing Neighbors: Webs of Violence in Rwanda*. Ithaca, NY: Cornell University Press, 2009.

Gellately, Robert, and Ben Kiernan, eds. *The Specter of Genocide: Mass Murder in Historical Perspective*. New York: Cambridge University Press, 2003.

Gourevitch, Philip. "Among the Dead." *Disturbing Remains: Memory, History, and Crisis in the Twentieth Century*, edited by Michael S. Roth and Charles G. Salas, 63–76. Los Angeles: Getty Research Institute, 2001.

Gourevitch, Philip. *We Wish to Inform You That Tomorrow We Will Be Killed with Our Families: Stories from Rwanda*. New York: Farrar, Straus, and Giroux, 1998.

Hatzfeld, Jean. *Life Laid Bare: The Survivors in Rwanda Speak*. Trans. Linda Coverdale. New York: Farrar, Straus and Giroux, 2006.

Hatzfeld, Jean. *Machete Season: The Killers in Rwanda Speak: A Report*. New York: Farrar, Straus and Giroux, 2005.

Hatzfeld, Jean. *The Antelope's Strategy: Living in Rwanda after the Genocide*. New York: Farrar, Straus and Giroux, 2009.

Ilibagiza, Immaculée, and Steve Erwin. *Left to Tell: Discovering God amidst the Rwandan Holocaust*. Carlsbad, CA: Hay House, 2006.

Jensen, Hanna. *Over a Thousand Hills I Walk with You*. Trans. Elizabeth D. Crawford. Minneapolis: Carolrhoda, 2006.

Jones, Adam. "Holocaust in Rwanda." In *Genocide: A Comprehensive Introduction*, 2nd ed., 232–257. New York: Routledge, 2011.

Kimenyi, Alexandre, and Otis L. Scott, eds. *Anatomy of Genocide: State-Sponsored Mass-Killings in the Twentieth Century*. Lewiston, NY: E. Mellen, 2002.

Kinzer, Stephen. *A Thousand Hills: Rwanda's Rebirth and the Man Who Dreamed It*. Hoboken, NJ: John Wiley & Sons, 2008.

List, Garrett, comp. *Rwanda 94: An Attempt at Symbolic Reparation to the Dead, For Use by the Living*. Brussels: Carbon 7 Records, 2000.

Longman, Timothy. *Christianity and Genocide in Rwanda*. New York: Cambridge University Press, 2010.

Mamdani, Mahmood. *When Victims Become Killers: Colonialism, Nativism, and the Genocide in Rwanda*. Princeton, NJ: Princeton University Press, 2001.

McCullum, Hugh. *The Angels Have Left Us: The Rwanda Tragedy and the Churches*. Geneva: WCC Publications, 1995.

Melvern, Linda. *A People Betrayed: The Role of the West in Rwanda's Genocide*. 2nd ed. London: Zed Books, 2009.

Melvern, Linda. *Conspiracy to Murder: The Rwandan Genocide*. London: Verso, 2004.

Mugesera, Antoine. *The Persecution of Rwandan Tutsi before the 1990–1994 Genocide*. Kigali: Rwanda Printery Company, Ltd., 2014

Mvuyekure, Pierre-Damien. *Lamentations on the Rwandan Genocide: Poems*. Cedar Falls, IA: Final Thursday Press, 2006.

Oosterom, Wiljo Woodi, ed. *Stars of Rwanda: Children Write and Draw about Their Experiences during the Genocide of 1994*. Kigali: Silent Work Foundation, 2004.

Power, Samantha. *A Problem from Hell: America and the Age of Genocide*. New York: Basic Books, 2002.

Prunier, Gérard. *The Rwanda Crisis: History of a Genocide*. New York: Columbia University Press, 1997.

Ranck, Jody. "Beyond Reconciliation: Memory and Alterity in Post-Genocide Rwanda." In *Between Hope and Despair: Pedagogy and the Remembrance of Historical Trauma*. Ed. Roger I. Simon, Sharon Rosenberg, and Claudia Eppert, 187–211. Lanham: Rowman & Littlefield, 2000.

Rwanda National Commission for the Fight against Genocide. *15 Years after the Genocide Perpetrated against Tutsi (1994-2009): Challenges and Prospects = 15 Ans Après Le Génocide Perpétré Contre Les Tutsi (1994–2009): Défis Et Perspectives*, 149–157. Kigali: Republic of Rwanda, National Commission for the Fight against Genocide, 2010.

Saul, Jack. *Collective Trauma, Collective Healing*. New York: Routledge, 2014.

Sebarenzi, Joseph, and Laura Mullane. *God Sleeps in Rwanda: A Journey of Transformation*. New York: Atria, 2009.

Shattered Lives: Sexual Violence during the Rwandan Genocide and Its Aftermath. New York: Human Rights Watch, 1996.

Snyder, Timothy. *Bloodlands: Europe Between Hitler and Stalin*. New York: Basic Books, 2010.

Stassen, Jean-Philippe. *Deogratias, A Tale of Rwanda*. New York: First Second, 2006.

Tuhabonye, Gilbert, with Gary Brozek. *This Voice in My Heart: A Genocide Survivor's Story of Escape, Faith, and Forgiveness.* New York: Amistad, 2006.

Voices of Rwanda. South Africa: JAM International, 2003.

Wallis, Andrew. *Silent Accomplice: The Untold Story of France's Role in the Rwandan Genocide.* London: I. B. Tauris, 2014.

Whitworth, Wendy, ed. *We Survived Genocide in Rwanda.* Nottinghamshire, UK: Quill, 2006.

Film

100 Days. Dir. Nick Hughes. Prod. Eric Kabera and Nick Hughes. Vivid Features, 2001.

As We Forgive. Dir. Laura Waters Hinson. Prod. Stephen McEveety. Image Bearer Pictures, 2009.

Beyond the Gates. Dir. Michael Caton-Jones. 20th Century Fox, 2004.

Gacaca, Living Together in Rwanda. Dir. Anne Aghion. Prod. Philip Brooks, Laurent Bocahut, and Anne Aghion. Dominant 7, Gacaca Productions, Planete, 2002.

Ghosts of Rwanda. Dir. Greg Barker. PBS, 2004.

Hotel Rwanda. Dir. Terry George. Lions Gate Entertainment, 2004.

In Rwanda We Say . . . The Family That Does Not Speak Dies. Dir. Anne Aghion. Prod. Laurent Bocahut. Gacaca Productions, Incarus Films, 2004.

In the Tall Grass: Inside the Citizen-based Justice System Gacaca. Dir. J. Coll Metcalfe. Prod. Eugene Cornelius. Choices, Inc., 2006.

My Neighbor My Killer. Dir. Anne Aghion. Prod. Anne Aghion. Gacaca Productions, 2009.

Sometimes in April. Dir. Raoul Peck. HBO Studios, 2005.

The Notebooks of Memory. Dir. Anne Aghion. Prod. Anne Aghion. Gacaca Productions, 2009.

ACKNOWLEDGMENTS

This work took place over nearly a decade, and it is impossible for me to acknowledge adequately all those who deserve my thanks. Let me apologize in advance for accidental oversights—my gratitude is more far-reaching than my memory.

First and foremost, I am indebted to the Rwandans who have shared with me their stories and their lives. In particular, I want to express my immense gratitude to Rose Mukankaka and Glorieuse Uwizeye, who from the start were convinced of the healing power of writing and the importance of doing this work. Mama Rose is a force for good in the world; her love for and commitment to the children of Rwanda is beyond words. Glori has been steadfast in her support—believing in this project every step of the way, even when there were long silences and unexpected turns; introducing me in ever more detail to the complex history and culture of Rwanda; answering questions, questions, and more questions with deep knowing and unflagging good humor.

Ernest Mutwarasibo, Louise Mukamwezi, Emery Ndoli, Emmanuel Kwizera, and Françoise (Fanny) Nishimwe are true heroes, each one. They made themselves vulnerable, they opened their hearts, they took a great leap of faith into words. I am guided by their extraordinary courage, their vision, and the strength of their light. *Namaste.*

I wish to thank Michigan State University for institutional support of this work. The original writing-for-healing project was launched with the help of an MSU International Development Research Initiative Grant; transcription of survivor interviews and narratives was made possible through a grant from the Frank and Adelaide Kussy Memorial Scholarship. The College of Education and an MSU Special Foreign Travel Fund allowed me to present early versions of the writing-for-healing project in Kigali at the International Symposium on the Genocide against Tutsi.

When the poems took center stage, I was awarded a grant through the MSU Intramural Research Grant Program, which allowed me to spend stretches of time writing poetry in Rwanda. At the conclusion of the work, an MSU Teacher Education faculty fellowship made it possible for me to return to Rwanda to share my poems with my colleagues there, and later to participate in The International Forum on Genocide and Kwibuka20. More importantly, I was provided sabbatical release time to do much of this writing. Over the years, I had the good fortune to work with administrators who granted me freedom to go where my heart called: department chair Mary Lundeberg provided funds and encouragement at the start of the work; department chair Suzanne Wilson supported my travel, cleared time for me to write, and nurtured this work to its conclusion. Jack Schwille, assistant dean for international studies in education, bolstered me when things seemed hard. Dean Carole Ames believed a poet could have a home in a college of education, and for that I will always be grateful.

I must, of course, recognize the U.S. partners with whom I embarked on the original writing-for-healing project: Ken Bialek, Tatyana Sigal, and Yakov Sigal, along with Frank Biocca, who served as a translator when participant interviews were conducted in French and who cheered me into the home stretch.

Many of these poems were completed at writing residencies: The Banff Centre for the Arts, where Stan Dragland convinced me that the early writings held some poetry inside; The Hambidge Center for the Arts (thank you, Deb and Ron Sanders, for all you do to keep the place going, and for welcoming me again and again); and the Virginia Center for the Creative Arts, where the snowy fields seemed impossibly far from, yet inexplicably close to the rolling hills of Rwanda.

Along the way, I have benefitted from the expertise and wisdom of many good readers; their thoughtful feedback sent me back to the manuscript, again and again. Often they understood better than I did where the work was trying to go, and they helped me avoid many of the mistakes I seemed determined to make. This collection could not have come into being without them: Melanie Morrison, Chris Root and David Wiley, Stephanie Alnot, Al and Priscilla Clemente, Jesse Obbink, Janine Certo, and Anita Skeen. My Rwandan colleagues read and provided feedback on late versions of the manuscript as well: Glori, Ernest, Emery, Louise, Emmanuel, Rose, and Samuel Byiringiro. It goes without saying that although these colleagues and friends did their best to teach and guide me, there remain inevitable misunderstandings and errors; for those I alone am to blame.

I have been blessed with good friends who held my hand when I was far away, overwhelmed, and feeling very much alone in this work: Carol Mason-Straughan, Stephanie Jordan, Cynthia Hockett, Scott Harris, and Cathy Colando-Riley. Those phone calls, across continents, were a lifeline. Jeanne Alnot helped me turn ramblings into essays; Hanna Obbink turned a stack of books into a bibliography and made a lot of airport runs to see me off and bring me home. Sue Clark kept my environment orderly so I could write, and Karen Gray made sure I had what I needed while I was away. The staff at Heaven, the restaurant and guesthouse in Kigali, always greeted me with a smile—especially Charles, Louise, Solange, and Rose.

It is no small feat to turn a sheaf of poems into a finished book. Thank you to Gabriel Dotto, director of the Michigan State University Press, who shepherded the manuscript from idea to publication with wisdom and vision, to the excellent editors who smoothed the rough edges, and to Fern Seiden, a friend from the Virginia Center for the Arts, who created the artwork for the cover as an act of love—not only for me, but also for the people she met on these pages.

I am grateful to my father, Dallas Apol, who passed on to me a passion for stories and poems; and to my mother, Gladys, who modeled a heart that listens, and who worried about me while I was away. I wish she could see that I have followed this through to the end. She knew I would.

My biggest thanks I have saved for last: David Pimm. Every step of the way, he kept me steady, hand on the wheel. He helped me see the poems in the poems, the structure in the disorder, the book in the myriad drafts. More than anyone, he believed in this project and in my ability to do it. Though he never set foot in Rwanda, he was there all along. Thank you, my dear poet friend.